# THE LATE MR. SHERLOCK HOLMES
*and other literary studies*

"Nothing remained of the heap of shag" (*see p.* 121)

# THE LATE MR. SHERLOCK HOLMES

## *& Other Literary Studies*

TREVOR H. HALL

ST MARTIN'S PRESS

NEW YORK

AFFILIATED PUBLISHERS: *Macmillan & Company Limited,*
*London – also at Bombay, Calcutta, Madras, and Melbourne –*
*The Macmillan Company of Canada Limited, Toronto*

# PREFACE

I<small>T</small> is my pleasant duty to acknowledge the assistance I have received in the preparation of this book, and gratefully to record the willingness of other writers and their publishers to allow me to quote from the existing literature.

My thanks are due, and are gladly rendered, to the late Adrian Conan Doyle and the Sir Arthur Conan Doyle Estates for permitting me to write about Sherlock Holmes, and to Messrs. John Murray for allowing me to quote from their editions of the stories and to make extracts from the original text of *The Strand Magazine*. The Oxford University Press, with the kind consent of Lady Roberts, has once again permitted me to quote from the late Sir Sydney Roberts's *Holmes & Watson. A Miscellany*, and my renewed thanks are due to Messrs. George Allen & Unwin Ltd. and the Estate of the late Gavin Brend for allowing me to extract a paragraph or so from *My Dear Holmes. A Study in Sherlock*. I am indebted to the same publishers and to Mr. James Edward Holroyd for allowing me to quote from *Seventeen Steps to 221 B*. I am grateful to Messrs. Constable and Company Limited and to the Estate of the late Harold W. Bell for again permitting me to use extracts from *Baker Street Studies* and *Sherlock Holmes & Dr. Watson. The Chronology of their Adventures*.

Messrs. Granada Publishing Limited and Messrs. Rupert Hart-Davis Limited have kindly allowed me to quote from the late W. S. Baring-Gould's text of *Sherlock Holmes. A Biography of the World's First Consulting Detective*, and similar permission has been given on behalf of the owner of the copyright by Messrs. A. P. Watt & Son. I have used a few sentences from *Essays in Satire* with the kind consent of the Literary Executor of the late Monsignor Ronald A. Knox, Messrs. Sheed & Ward and Messrs. A. P. Watt & Son, and from the late Dorothy L. Sayers's *Unpopular Opinions* with the permission of Messrs.

David Higham Associates Ltd., the author's executors and Messrs. Victor Gollancz Ltd.

I am grateful to Mr. Thomas S. Blakeney for allowing me to quote from our correspondence and from *Sherlock Holmes: Fact or Fiction?*, and this acknowledgement includes his agents and his publishers, Messrs. Christy & Moore Ltd. and Messrs. John Murray. I am indebted to Mr. Vincent Starrett for his kind consent to my making a short extract from *The Private Life of Sherlock Holmes* and to the Editor of the *Sherlock Holmes Journal*, the Marquis of Donegall, and the Sherlock Holmes Society of London, for renewed permission to use material from that publication. If I have inadvertently omitted any acknowledgement which is due, my apologies are tendered in advance.

I am especially indebted to Miss Madeleine B. Stern, whose essay on Holmes's library aroused my own interest in his supposed status as a book-collector. The book would have been noticeably the poorer without the many kind and constructive suggestions of John Horden, the Director of the Institute of Bibliography and Textual Criticism at the University of Leeds, D. G. Neill of the Bodleian Library, Hartley Thwaite of the Yorkshire Archaeological Society and Eric J. Dingwall of the British Museum. My obligation to Dr. Dingwall is the greater because of his amiable disapproval of the whole subject and my involvement in it. My special thanks are due to my secretary, Mrs. Susan Spriggs, who has given much care to the preparation and checking of the typescript.          T.H.H.

# CONTENTS

# LIST OF ILLUSTRATIONS

# ABBREVIATED REFERENCES

## THE CANON

S.                     *The Complete Sherlock Holmes Short Stories* (London, 1928).

L.                     *The Complete Sherlock Holmes Long Stories* (London, 1929).

## GENERAL REFERENCES

*Baker Street Studies.*   H. W. Bell (Ed.), *Baker Street Studies. A Miscellany of Sherlockian material by* Dorothy L. Sayers, Helen Simpson, Vernon Rendall, Vincent Starrett, Ronald A. Knox, A. G. MacDonnell, S. C. Roberts and H. W. Bell (London 1934).

Baring-Gould.   William S. Baring-Gould, *Sherlock Holmes. A Biography of the World's First Consulting Detective* (London, 1962).

Blakeney.   Thomas S. Blakeney, *Sherlock Holmes: Fact or Fiction?* (London, 1932).

Brend.   Gavin Brend, *My Dear Holmes. A Study in Sherlock* (London, 1951).

*Chronology.*   H. W. Bell, *Sherlock Holmes and Dr. Watson. The Chronology of Their Adventures* (London, 1932).

Hall.   Trevor H. Hall, *Sherlock Holmes. Ten Literary Studies* (London, 1969).

Roberts.   S. C. Roberts, *Holmes & Watson. A Miscellany* (London, 1953).

*SHJ*   *The Sherlock Holmes Journal.* Edited by the Marquis of Donegall and published by the Sherlock Holmes Society of London.

Starrett.   Vincent Starrett, *The Private Life of Sherlock Holmes* London, 1934).

# INTRODUCTION

I THINK of writing another little monograph", remarked Mr. Sherlock Holmes to James Windibank at the conclusion of the affair of Miss Mary Sutherland's vanishing bridegroom in September, 1888.[1] That this was a serious statement of intent is demonstrated by the far from casual context, for Holmes was about to terminate his conversation with Windibank (alias Hosmer Angel) by reaching for his hunting crop and causing his visitor to "run at the top of his speed down the road".

Only two months previously, the great detective had confessed to Dr. Watson that he was already responsible for three other works, dealing with the distinction between 140 varieties of tobacco-ash, the tracing of footsteps and the influence of vocations upon the form of the hand.[2] Holmes was perhaps unduly modest about his literary achievements to Watson in July, 1888, for we know from his own contemporary account to his biographer as early as 1881 that he had published at that time a long, anonymous magazine article, "The Book of Life", on the science of observation, deduction and analysis.[3] Perhaps the fact that Watson had thoughtlessly described it as "ineffable twaddle" and "rubbish" was the reason why Holmes refrained from any mention of "The Book of Life" in 1888.[4] Watson had subsequently modified his opinion of his friend's work, in the face of Holmes's practical demonstration of his methods by the accurate identification of a commissionaire, temporarily out of uniform, as a retired sergeant of Marines.[5] It may be thought, however, in the light of Holmes's proud nature,[6] that the initial, spontaneous criticism still rankled.

It seems very possible, too, that Holmes had "contributed to the literature of the subject" of tattoo marks[7] whilst still an

---

[1] *A Case of Identity*, S., p. 71.    [2] *The Sign of Four*, L., p. 147.
[3] *A Study in Scarlet*, L., pp. 19–20.    [4] *Ibid.*, p. 21.    [5] *Ibid*, p. 24.
[6] *The Sussex Vampire*, S., p. 1180, and *The Norwood Builder*, S., p. 584.
[7] *The Red-Headed League*, S., p. 32.

1

undergraduate at Trinity College, Cambridge. It is true that he did not acknowledge until 1889 to Watson and Mr. Jabez Wilson that he had written this article or monograph, but Holmes's obvious interest in the tattooing of the arm of "Justice of the Peace Trevor" at Donnithorpe in Norfolk in 1873 suggests that he may have been preoccupied with the subject at that time.[1]

Holmes's literary output was both versatile and considerable. He contributed two important articles upon the anatomical peculiarities of the human ear to the *Anthropological Journal*,[2] whilst his monograph on the dating of documents had a sufficiently wide circulation for him to assume that Dr. James Mortimer would have read it.[3] His important work on secret writings analysed no less than 160 separate ciphers, despite his modest description of it as "a trifling monograph".[4] His erudite study of the Polyphonic Motets of [de] Lassus, undertaken at the request of Queen Victoria,[5] was naturally printed for private circulation only, but it was "said by experts to be the last word on the subject."[6] Holmes's two published autobiographical accounts of the cases of *The Blanched Soldier* and *The Lion's Mane* are, of course, well known. His last work, written in his retirement on the South Downs, was "a small blue book", which Holmes described affectionately as his *magnum opus*, "the fruit of pensive nights and laborious days". Its gilt-lettered title was *Practical Handbook of Bee Culture, with some Observations upon the Segregation of the Queen.*[7]

This brief account of Holmes's literary work[8] makes it clear that the description "a man of letters", which he conferred upon Watson "with a mischievous twinkle in his eyes",[9] was fully applicable to himself. His pen, moreover, was a restless one.

[1] *The "Gloria Scott"*, L., p. 378.
[2] *The Cardboard Box*, S., p. 937.    [3] *The Hound of the Baskervilles*, L., p. 282.
[4] *The Dancing Men*, S., p. 630.
[5] For the documentation of this assertion, see Hall, pp. 88–91.
[6] *The Bruce-Partington Plans*, S., p. 1000. I suspect that all the monographs were printed for private circulation, for none of them are included in the *Subject Index of the Modern Works added to the Library of the British Museum in the Years* 1881–1900 (3 vols., London, 1902–3) edited by G. K. Fortescue.
[7] *His Last Bow*, S., p. 1082.
[8] In his "A Bibliography of Sherlock Holmes" (*Dr. Watson*, pp. 31–2) Sir Sydney Roberts omitted to include the monograph on secret writings, the two articles on the human ear and "The Book of Life".    [9] *Wisteria Lodge*, S., p. 891.

Full of ideas, he was forever planning new books on other subjects, although most unfortunately the text of the canon does not contain any record of their actual publication. I have already mentioned his expressed determination to James Windibank to write "another little monograph", which was to be on the typewriter and its relation to crime. Holmes told Watson that he had "serious thoughts" of preparing studies on the uses of dogs in detective work[1] and on the subject of malingering.[2] Most importantly of all, perhaps, was his expressed determination to Watson during the case of the murder of Sir Eustace Brackenstall (whose "head was knocked in with his own poker") to devote some of his retirement "to the composition of a textbook which shall focus the whole art of detection into one volume."[3]

The assembly of the evidence demonstrating that throughout the whole of his professional life and his years of retirement Holmes could never resist the temptation to add to his existing literary work, provides me with an absolute canonical precedent for offering a second collection of Baker Street studies.[4] I am once more tossing my deerstalker in the ring, and renewing the hope contained in the last sentence of my earlier Introduction— that the other exponents of the Higher Criticism of the literature of Sherlock Holmes, most of whose conclusions I have questioned, will spring upon me "like so many staghounds".[5]

My reference to the deerstalker is inspired by the challenge attributed to Theodore Roosevelt at a newspaper interview on 21 February, 1912, at Cleveland, Ohio, "My hat's in the ring. The fight is on and I'm stripped to the buff." A deerstalker is considered to be the appropriate hat for a Sherlockian today, although this tradition is not supported by the Sidney Paget

[1] *The Creeping Man*, S., p. 1245.    [2] *The Dying Detective*, S., p. 1017.
[3] *The Abbey Grange*, S., p. 834.
[4] In this connexion it is noteworthy that on the first page of the text of the second volume of his *Bibliographical Notes on Histories of Inventions and Books of Secrets* (First Collected Edition, 2 vols., London, 1959), the late Professor John Ferguson explained the reason for the later series of his published lectures to the Glasgow Archaeological Society. "I have found that the subject would not rest, but kept itself in evidence whether I wished it or not." As it can scarcely be seriously suggested that mere bibliographical inquiry can approach, either in importance or scope, the study of the corpus of the literature of Baker Street and the investigation of the lives of Holmes and Watson, no excuse is required for the recording of new discoveries in the latter field.
[5] *A Study in Scarlet*, L., p. 72.

illustrations of the first editions of *The Adventures, The Memoirs* and *The Hound of the Baskervilles*. Of 47 drawings of Holmes wearing a hat, 16 show him wearing a bowler, 13 a trilby, 10 a deerstalker, 7 a top hat, and on one occasion only, a boater. The deerstalker's third place, moreover, relies in part upon four illustrations from *Silver Blaze*, where in the text Holmes's headgear, by contrast, is described as "his ear-flapped travelling-cap."[1] Perhaps the choice of the deerstalker is partly sentimental, and stems from the frontispiece of *The Memoirs*, "The Death of Sherlock Holmes", in which the deerstalker is to be seen falling into the "dreadful cauldron" of the Reichenbach.

One of the circumstances upon which I relied to qualify me to write about Sherlock Holmes was that in the words of James E. Holroyd I was "so to speak, built into the saga". This referred, of course, to my first forename, the fact that I am a magistrate and to "the message which struck Justice of the Peace Trevor dead with horror when he read it".[2] As it may be suggested that this qualification was expended by the publication of my earlier book, I have naturally searched for other coincidences that connect my family or myself with the Baker Street canon. I have found two, the first of which offers a small mystery which I have been unable to solve.

My grandmother, Anne Elizabeth Roxby Hall (1851–1932), kept a small book, "Memorandum of Special Events", which was quite distinct from her many diaries. In it she recorded births, marriages and deaths, family gatherings, the departure of her three sons to school, university and World War I, holidays, the employment of new maids,[3] the Lord Mayor's Ball, visits to the opera, the death of the King[4] and other matters which she regarded as of special interest and importance to her. At Easter, 1903, she was on holiday at Llandudno with my grandfather. The entry which I find of extreme interest is as follows:

"Sat. April 11. By steamer to Bangor—Menai Bridge. Back to L. by train. Lovely Sherlock Holmes evening."

There is no mention of Holmes anywhere else in the "Memoran-

---

[1] *Silver Blaze*, S., p. 306.    [2] *The "Gloria Scott"*, S., p. 374.
[3] And on one occasion, a departure. "My maid A—— in trouble; leaving to be married (*perhaps*)."    [4] 6 May, 1910.

dum". My grandparents were in the habit of reading aloud to each other, but this is the only possible occasion recorded in the "Memorandum" of this vanished and graceful pastime. My guess is that this is what the entry means, but I remain puzzled as to why the reading aloud of a Sherlock Holmes story in a Llandudno hotel should have been a "special event" on 11 April, 1903, to a lady of 52.

The date is of no canonical significance. In March, 1902 *The Hound of the Baskervilles* was published by Newnes,. and in October of the same year *A Study in Scarlet* was re-issued by Ward Lock & Co.[1] 1903 was, however, a blank year for Sherlockians until that glorious day in the autumn when "The Adventure of the Empty House" was published in *The Strand Magazine* for October, and the news that Holmes was alive and back with Watson in Baker Street caused queues to form at the bookstalls. I do not know, therefore, any special reason for that "lovely Sherlock Holmes evening" enjoyed by my grandmother nearly seventy years ago. I must be content with the pleasure of recording it.

The second coincidence is so remarkable that I have thought it prudent to check my recollection of events of nearly forty years ago, and to express my obligation to the Clerk to Horsforth Urban District Council at the Council Offices, Manor Road, Horsforth, near Leeds, who has kindly looked at his records to make sure that my memory has not deceived me. When my years of formal education were over and I began my training as a chartered surveyor, I learnt the practical art of valuation with a firm specialising in the preparation of rating assessments and valuation lists for small local authorities, under the provisions of the Rating and Valuation Act, 1925. I was at one of the Yorkshire offices, and in the course of my work in 1933 I had to inspect and value every property in the area of Horsforth U.D.C.[2] I naturally spent much time in the Council Offices, and came to know well the officials of those days.

---

[1] *The English Catalogue of Books*, London, 1906, vii, January 1901 to December 1905, p. 315.

[2] An old tradition among surveyors engaged upon this kind of work, involving entering every house in a district, is that the simple law of averages will ensure at least one encounter with a nymphomaniac among the housewives, and at least one bite from a savage dog.

The Clerk to the Council in 1933, who signed the authority for me to enter all properties in the district, was Mr. L. W. Sherlock. The Deputy Clerk to the Council and Chief Rating Officer was Mr. Hudson Holmes. The Assistant Rating Officer was Mr. E. ("Teddy") Watson. It is, therefore, a matter of historical fact that the persons in a small Council Office who were of the greatest help to the future "Justice of the Peace Trevor" in his earliest professional work in 1933 were Sherlock, Holmes and Watson![1]

The pattern of the present collection of literary studies follows that of the first. I am a Holmesian fundamentalist, and the evidence upon which the arguments rely is, therefore, based upon the text of the canon, which must be the absolute authority. External facts, which can occasionally be relevant, are only acceptable if they support what Sherlockians in America call the Sacred Writings. If they do not, then we are entitled to suspect that there is something wrong with them.

As regards the first point, commentators who recklessly tamper with the canon create serious difficulties for themselves. The late Gavin Brend, for example, in order to justify his view that the events in *The Valley of Fear* must have taken place not earlier than 1900,[2] nine years after *The Final Problem* (which according to the text of the canon was the *later* case of the two) was forced to advance the outrageous suggestion that Holmes's story to Watson of his journeying through Tibet and elsewhere between 1891 and 1894, when he was presumed to be dead, was pure invention.[3] The facts are, in Watson's own words, that the mystery of Birlstone, recorded in *The Valley of Fear*, took place in "the early days at the end of the eighties, when [Inspector] Alec MacDonald was far from having attained the national fame which he has now achieved. He was a young but trusted member of the detective force".[4] Since the action of the

---

[1] It will be recalled that Hudson was the name of both Holmes's housekeeper and the villain of The "*Gloria Scott*". As this is written (24 June, 1970) both the BBC and *The Times* (on the front page under the heading "Elementary, my dear Wilson") are making much of the fact that among the neighbours of the former Socialist Prime Minister in Vincent Square, Westminster, are a Mr. Sherlock and a Mr. Holmes.
[2] Brend, p. 112. Bell (*Chronology*, p. 33) and Blakeney (p. 75) respectively date *The Valley of Fear* as 1887 and 1890.
[3] Brend, p. 121.
[4] *The Valley of Fear*, L., p. 467.

case started on 7 January[1] and Watson was still living at Baker Street at the time, it is clear that the most appropriate date "at the end of the 'eighties", was 7 January, 1888, some months before Watson's engagement to Mary Morstan in July, 1888[2] and his subsequent marriage.

Even so simple a calculation as this is not necessary in the dating of *The Final Problem*, for Watson tells us simply and firmly that Holmes's visit to him at the very start of the case was "upon the evening of the 24th April" and that it was the April of "the early spring of 1891".[3] The chronology of *The Valley of Fear* (7 January, 1888) and *The Final Problem* (24 April, 1891) is therefore solidly established so far as the fundamentalist is concerned.

It is true that a slight problem presents itself if Watson's comments upon Professor Moriarty during these cases are compared. On 7 January, 1888, the following exchange took place at Baker Street between Holmes and Watson:

" 'You have heard me speak of Professor Moriarty?'

'The famous scientific criminal, as famous among crooks as——'.

'My blushes, Watson,' Holmes murmured, in a deprecating voice.

'I was about to say "as he is unknown to the public".'

'A touch—a distinct touch!' cried Holmes. 'You are developing a certain unexpected vein of pawky humour, Watson, against which I must learn to guard myself. But in calling Moriarty a criminal you are uttering libel in the eyes of the law, and there lies the glory and the wonder of it . . . Foul-mouthed doctor and slandered professor—such would be your respective rôles.' "[4]

Brend found difficulty in reconciling this with Watson's answer to a question by Holmes three years later on the evening of 24 April, 1891, at the beginning of the action of *The Final Problem*:

" 'You have probably never heard of Professor Moriarty?' said he.

[1] *The Valley of Fear*, p. 466. " 'We pay the price, Watson, for being too up-to-date', he cried. 'We are before our time, and suffer the usual penalties. Being the seventh of January, we have very properly laid in the new almanack.' "
[2] *The Sign of Four*, L., pp. 154–5 and 270.   [3] *The Final Problem*, S., p. 537.
[4] *The Valley of Fear*, L., p. 460.

'Never.'

'Aye, there's the genius and wonder of the thing!' he cried. 'The man pervades London, and no one has heard of him. That's what puts him on a pinnacle in the records of crime.' "[1]

To the fundamentalist it must be obvious that Watson was simply suffering from a temporary aberration of memory about Moriarty in 1891. Holmes said on more than one occasion, "When you have excluded the impossible, whatever remains, however improbable, must be the truth."[2] Since it is clearly impossible that Holmes was a bare-faced liar, or that the canon is wrong in its dates, Watson's temporary failure of memory is the only reasonable explanation that remains. This solution, moreover, is not so improbable as it might appear at first sight. These were the first years of the euphoria of Watson's marriage to Mary Morstan, but on 24 April, 1891, Mrs. Watson was regrettably "away upon a visit" and Watson was alone.[3] In an essay in this book dealing with his married life I shall show that these absences of his wife were sufficiently disturbing to Watson to cause short lapses of memory. A comparison of two texts of *The Five Orange Pips*, for example, demonstrates that Watson could not accurately recall whether his wife was on a visit to her mother or her aunt,[4] whilst some commentators may suggest that Watson had even forgotten that Mary Morstan had no living relative in England.[5]

It is fair to recall, too, that Moriarty had been nothing more than a name to Watson during *The Valley of Fear* case in 1888. We may very reasonably suppose that his meeting with Mary Morstan so soon afterwards, to be followed by an ardent and extremely rapid courtship and marriage, would expunge more than a mere name from his mind. He said himself during this period:

"I had seen little of Holmes lately. My marriage had drifted us away from each other. My own complete happiness, and the home-centred interests which rise up around the man

[1] *The Final Problem*, S., pp. 538–9.   [2] *The Beryl Coronet*, S., p. 273.
[3] *The Final Problem*, S., p. 538.
[4] *The Five Orange Pips*, S., pp. 103–4, and *The Strand Magazine*, November, 1891, p. 481.
[5] *The Sign of Four*, L., p. 153.

who first finds himself master of his own establishment, *were sufficient to absorb all my attention.*" [my italics].[1]

It is proper to recall, too, that following his marriage, Watson had made a "subsequent start in private practice", and had assumed the cares and responsibilities of a busy physician.[2] There is no need to dwell further upon Watson's preoccupations, however, for the text of the canon fortunately provides us with a parallel example of his having completely forgotten, to Holmes's surprise, another well-known name:

> " 'The case worried me at the time, Watson. Here are my marginal notes to prove it. I confess that I could make nothing of it. And yet I was convinced that the coroner was wrong. Have you no recollection of the Abbas Parva tragedy?'
> 'None, Holmes.'
> 'And yet you were with me then . . . It will probably come back to your memory as I talk. Ronder, of course, was a household word.' "[3]

To the fundamentalist, any apparent contradiction of the canon by what the critic regards as facts should present no problem. As an example, the text informs us that when Holmes was an undergraduate Reginald Musgrave was a member of his college.[4] When I found that "R. Musgrave" appeared in *The Cambridge University Calendar* at the appropriate date I reproduced the evidence of the appropriate page photographically.[5] It would clearly have been improper of me, however, not to reveal, as I did, that in the Trinity College list this gentleman was oddly recorded as "Richard Musgrave".[6] The obvious (and indeed the only) explanation, of course, was that "Richard" was a misprint for "Reginald" by the publishers, Deighton, Bell and Co. and Bell and Daldy, a conclusion that I was able convincingly to document, by pointing to another example of a misprint by them in their publication of a book by Watson's uncle, G. C. Watson, M.D., in 1862.[7] This is an excellent example of what Sherlockian scholarship is all about.

---

[1] *A Scandal in Bohemia*, S., p. 3.
[3] *The Veiled Lodger*, S., p. 1291.
[5] Hall, Plate IVb.
[7] Hall, Plates Ia and Ib.

[2] *The Final Problem*, S., p. 537.
[4] *The Musgrave Ritual*, S., p. 399.
[6] Hall, p. 84.

I have taken the liberty of making reference to my earlier book in this way, because it is on this very point that I have an opportunity of offering a further exposition of the beliefs of the fundamentalist. I am exceedingly fortunate in the fact that my critic is my good friend Thomas S. Blakeney, whose knowledge of the literature of Sherlock Holmes is second to none. In the course of our correspondence Mr. Blakeney wrote:

"I must admit to being a bit unhappy over (p. 84) your identification of Reginald Musgrave with the R. Musgrave in *The Cambridge University Calendar* of 1870. I think that this lands you in the same difficulty as Dorothy Sayers's attempt to identify Holmes [as T. S. Holmes of Sidney Sussex], a point exploded by S. C. Roberts,[1] as you say (p. 77). I do not feel that this was unfair on Roberts's part, as you seem to imply; Dorothy Sayers had turned to official publications at Cambridge for her theory and could not reasonably object to Roberts doing the same. If one appeals to Caesar, one must allow Caesar to pass judgment.

I fear the same thing applies to Musgrave as to Holmes. Richard John Musgrave, at whom you are pointing, was the only son of Sir Richard Musgrave, Bart., of Tourin, Co. Waterford. Richard John Musgrave was born in December, 1850, at Waterford; succeeded his father as Bart. in 1874; was J.P. and D.L. for Co. Waterford in 1880, and died in 1930. (*see* Venn's *Alumni Cantab*). This will not fit in with Hurlstone, or with the description Holmes gives of the West Sussex Musgraves . . . Now is that not a case of trying to press Holmes-scholarship too far?"

In connexion with his first point, I reminded Mr. Blakeney that in my book I had recalled an evening in Sir Sydney's home in West Road, Cambridge, when I had been critical of this intrusion of facts into Miss Sayers's Sherlockian scholarship, and that Sir Sydney himself had generously agreed that he had perhaps been a trifle unchivalrous and hasty. He was possibly influenced towards this later and more enlightened view by some of the published comments, equally unfair, upon his own biographical research, and in particular his suggestion that Watson's mother might well have had Tractarian leanings, and

---

[1] Hall, p. 77. Sir Sydney Roberts had pointed out that T. S. Holmes of Sidney Sussex became Chancellor of Wells Cathedral (Roberts, p. 10).

therefore named her son "John Henry" after Newman.[1] H. W. Bell had unkindly pointed out that Newman had joined the Roman Church seven years before the putative date of Watson's birth.[2]

As regards Mr. Blakeney's second criticism, arising from his researches in Venn,[3] loyal Sherlockian fundamentalists will naturally share my conviction that the only acceptable explanation is that the compilers of these four large volumes were wrong about "R. Musgrave". In an immense work of this kind, it would be quite unreasonable to expect them not to make occasional mistakes.[4] I have admitted to Mr. Blakeney, however, that when I discovered that "R. Musgrave" had been at Trinity College, Cambridge, I did refer to Venn myself. This was, of course, merely out of curiosity, to see whether the compilers had obtained the correct information about Musgrave from the Baker Street canon, which was available to them at the time, or had mistakenly relied on less accurate sources, as unfortunately turned out to be the case. I have been frank to say to Mr. Blakeney, however, that I had a strong premonition that *Alumni Cantabrigienses* would be wrong even before I opened the appropriate volume. This feeling was so overwhelming that if the entry had indeed shown Musgrave as the squire of the manor of Hurlstone in Sussex and a college friend of Mr.

---

[1] Roberts, p. 64.　　　　　　　　　　　　　　[2] *Chronology*, p. 66.
[3] J. and J. A. Venn, *Alumni Cantabrigienses. A Biographical List of all known Students, Graduates and Holders of Office at the University of Cambridge, from the earliest times to 1900* (4 vols., Cambridge 1922–7).
[4] In a recent bibliographical study of Thomas Ady's *A Candle in the Dark* (London, 1655), with later editions of 1656 and 1661, I had occasion to assemble some details of Ady's life. The bare academic details that Ady was admitted to Emmanuel College, Cambridge, in 1624, obtained his bachelor's degree in 1627/8 and became an M.A. in 1631 were recorded correctly enough in Venn (Part I, i, p. 8). The compilers did not know, however, that Ady's book was first published in 1655, and mistakenly assumed that the second edition of 1656 was the *editio princeps*. They called it, moreover, *A Perfect Discovery of Witches*, which was the title of the *third* edition of 1661. They were entirely silent about the fact that Ady was an Essex man and succeeded his father as the squire of Wethersfield, and that he died on 19 February, 1672. To obtain this and other biographical information I had to seek the assistance of Dr. F. H. Stubbings, the Librarian of Emmanuel College, and Mr. F. G. Emmison, the Essex County Archivist. The title-page of the first edition of Ady's book was photographically reproduced as Plate I in my *A Bibliography of Books on Conjuring in English from 1580 to 1850* (Minneapolis, 1957). The printings of 1655, 1656 and 1661 were described on pp. 15–16, Nos. 5, 6 & 7. I have described them all as editions in this note for convenience, but *A Candle in the Dark*, 1656 and *A Perfect Discovery of Witches*, 1661, were in fact merely re-issues of the first edition of 1655, the title-pages being cancels.

Sherlock Holmes, later to become famous as the greatest consulting detective in the world, I think it probable that I should have shared a unique experience of Watson's. I have suggested to Mr. Blakeney that he might well have done the same.

"I rose to my feet . . . in utter amazement, and then it appears that I must have fainted for the first and the last time in my life. Certainly a grey mist swirled before my eyes, and when it cleared I found my collar-ends undone and the tingling after-taste of brandy upon my lips."[1]

Carr Meadow, Thorner, Yorkshire.                                    T.H.H.

[1] *The Empty House*, S., p. 564.

# I

# SHERLOCK HOLMES: ASCETIC OR GOURMET?

D<small>R</small>. W<small>ATSON</small> wrote of his friend Mr. Sherlock Holmes that "his diet was usually of the sparest, and his habits were simple to the verge of austerity".[1] Using the good doctor's own phrase in another context, it may be thought that this could be criticised as "rather a broad idea".[2] It seemed oddly to overlook the breakfasts offering either curried chicken or ham and eggs (or both), with toast, tea and coffee,[3] and to take no account of the leisurely and by no means austere luncheons through which the two friends "sat for an hour over a bottle of claret",[4] or of Beaune.[5] It seemed to ignore the dinners at Marcini's[6] and Simpson's (where Holmes and Watson indulged themselves on successive evenings during one case[7] and where at Holmes's own suggestion they sought "something nutritious" at the end of another[8]). Above all, Watson made no reference at all to the "quite epicurean little cold supper" at Baker Street when the two friends, assisted only by Mr. and Mrs. Francis Hay Moulton, sat down to enjoy "a couple of brace of cold woodcock, a pheasant, a *pâté-de-foie-gras* pie, with a group of ancient and cobwebby bottles".[9]

It may, of course, be urged that this apparent contradiction

---

[1] *The Yellow Face*, S., p. 334.     [2] *A Study in Scarlet*, L., p. 46.
[3] *The Naval Treaty*, S., p. 530. This was clearly not an unusual menu, for Holmes said of it with satisfaction that Mrs. Hudson had "as good an idea of breakfast as a Scotchwoman". (*Ibid.*, p. 530.)
[4] *The Cardboard Box*, S., p. 935. Holmes was unashamedly fond of claret. "I never needed it more", he said, as he refreshed himself with a glass on another occasion. (*The Dying Detective*, S., p. 1016.)
[5] *The Sign of Four*, L., p. 143.     [6] *The Hound of the Baskervilles*, L., p. 454.
[7] *The Illustrious Client*, S., pp. 1096 and 1102.
[8] *The Dying Detective*, S., p. 1018.     [9] *The Noble Bachelor*, S., p. 240.

is explained by Watson's qualification that his friend's diet "was *usually* [my italics] of the sparest", and that the quoted occasions suggesting the opposite were mainly concerned with gastronomic celebrations of the successful conclusion of difficult cases, exemplified by the consumption of a whole goose by the two friends at the end of the affair of Mr. James Ryder.[1] This would involve our believing that Watson really meant that it was during actual investigations that Holmes ate very little. There is some superficial support for this in the text, and even for Watson being convinced that on occasions, when faced with peculiarly intractable problems, his friend ate nothing at all. Watson recorded with anxiety, "I had very clear recollections of days and nights without a thought of food".[2]

That Watson was persuaded by Holmes that the latter's alleged fasting, or near fasting, was a necessary accompaniment to the successful detection of crime is demonstrated by Holmes's answer to an anxious question by his friend:

" 'But why not eat?'
'Because the faculties become refined when you starve them. Why, surely, as a doctor, my dear Watson, you must admit that what your digestion gains in the way of blood supply is so much lost to the brain. I am a brain, Watson. The rest of me is a mere appendix. Therefore, it is the brain I must consider.' "[3]

The doctor's concern over Holmes's abstinence, both as his physician and as a close friend, was very real. As he himself expressed it in another context, "You are knocking yourself up, old man".[4] It may be thought on the face of it that few would not share Watson's anxiety about his companion's health, an anxiety that would not be allayed by Holmes's frequent and flippant exhibitionism over his self-imposed denial:

" 'When will you be pleased to dine, Mr. Holmes?' Mrs. Hudson asked. 'Seven-thirty, the day after tomorrow', said he."[5]

The text makes it clear, however, that Watson accepted the situation, however much he may have disapproved of it:

[1] *The Blue Carbuncle*, S., p. 173.  [2] *The Valley of Fear*, L., p. 517.
[3] *The Mazarin Stone*, S., p. 1143.  [4] *The Sign of Four*, L., p. 218.
[5] *The Mazarin Stone*, S., p. 1141.

"My friend had no breakfast himself, for it was one of his peculiarities that in his more intense moments he would permit himself no food."[1]

I must say now that there is a good deal of evidence which does not support the neat theory contained in the foregoing paragraphs. During a crucial period of the investigation of "the very obscure circumstances which surrounded the death of Captain Peter Carey", for example, Holmes commented upon his own "excellent appetite" and gave a chuckle of an;icipation "as he poured out the coffee" at breakfast.[2] Holmes's indulgence in the pleasures of the first meal of the day was equally unaffected at a time almost precisely half-way through the intricacies of the Sholto mystery, with Holmes "grinning over his coffee cup" to the accompaniment of ham and eggs at Baker Street.[3] In the thick of the puzzling business of "the professor, it was she" Holmes did not refuse a substantial luncheon of cutlets at Yoxley Old Place, even after spending the morning "consuming cigarette after cigarette" from Professor Coram's large private supply specially imported from Alexandria.[4] Immediately prior to the crisis of the sombre affair of the severed human ears Holmes felt in urgent need of his midday intake of well-cooked and well served food:

"Drive us to some decent hotel, cabby, where we may have some lunch."

The order was obeyed, and the friends enjoyed "a pleasant little meal" together,[5] during which Holmes told Watson how he had bought his Stradivarius for fifty-five shillings in Tottenham Court Road, and regaled him with anecdotes of Paganini.

It is odd that a man who was supposed to refrain from eating in order to assist his intellectual effort should have regarded tea as a serious meal. With the Birlstone mystery in full swing, (124 pages before the end of Watson's account of it, in fact) Holmes attacked a high tea "with a ravenous appetite", and "with his mouth full of toast", consumed no less than four eggs.[6]

[1] *The Norwood Builder*, S., p. 600.      [2] *Black Peter*, S., pp. 697–8.
[3] *The Sign of Four*, L., pp. 211–12.
[4] *The Golden Pince-Nez*, S., pp. 797, 799 and 800.
[5] *The Cardboard Box*, S., p. 935.        [6] *The Valley of Fear*, L., p. 516.

At a crisis in the affair of Irene Adler and the hereditary King of Bohemia, when Holmes admitted to Watson that he found "his plans very seriously menaced", he said that the only course open to him was "to make my own arrangements".

" 'Which are?' [asked Watson]

'Some cold beef and a glass of beer', he answered." When the tray was brought in, Holmes "turned hungrily upon the simple fare that our landlady had provided".[1] The mystery of the disappearance of Mr. Neville St. Clair was not nearly solved when Holmes and Watson accepted Mrs. St. Clair's hospitable offer of "a large and comfortable double-bedded room" at The Cedars at Lee "because", as Holmes said, "there are many inquiries which must be made out here". Before those inquiries could be prosecuted, however, there was a necessary preliminary which Holmes clearly regarded as of importance. "We shall now have a little supper and then retire, for we may have a very busy day tomorrow".[2]

It is of additional interest to recall that in the middle of the Cadogan West affair Holmes invited Watson to join him for dinner at Goldini's Restaurant in Gloucester Road, bringing with him "a jemmy, a dark lantern, a chisel, and a revolver". Watson obeyed this summons, but it may be presumed that the assembly of this collection of unusual equipment took more time than the hungry Holmes was prepared to wait for dinner, for he had finished his meal when Watson arrived at "the garish Italian restaurant". The doctor was offered nothing more substantial than a coffee, a curaçao and "one of the proprietor's cigars", which Holmes kindly assured him were "less poisonous than one would expect".[3] In view of this disappointment, it is pleasant to record that Watson fared much better in the Abbas Parva tragedy. At the most difficult stage in the investigation, when Holmes said that "our speculations are futile until we have

---

[1] *A Scandal in Bohemia*, S., pp. 18–19. It speaks well for the imperturbability of the two friends that neither betrayed the slightest surprise when on this single occasion in the entire canon the tray was brought in by a "Mrs. Turner", who must have been a complete stranger to both of them. Who this lady was we shall probably never know. She apparently came from nowhere and seems never to have been seen again. The landlady at Baker Street was, of course, Mrs. Martha Hudson.

[2] *The Man with the Twisted Lip*, S., pp. 137 and 142.

[3] *The Bruce-Partington Plans*, S., pp. 989–90.

all the facts", the hungry Watson might have expected that the chance of a civilised meal was indeed remote. He must have been very agreeably surprised by Holmes's remarks that immediately followed:

> "There is a cold partridge on the sideboard, Watson, and a bottle of Montrachet. Let us renew our energies before we make a fresh call upon them."[1]

It is surprising that Watson should have been bamboozled by Holmes into believing in the patent fiction that the great detective was in the habit of starving himself during investigations in order to sharpen his intellectual powers, in view of the wealth of incidents in which Watson was involved which prove the opposite. In the middle of the urgent search for Godfrey Staunton, "the crack three-quarter, Cambridge, Blackheath, and five Internationals", a frustrated and dejected Holmes was unwilling to tell Watson how he had been foiled by Dr. Leslie Armstrong (whom Holmes considered to be the equal of Professor Moriarty) until, after a cold supper, "his needs were satisfied and his pipe alight".[2] Perhaps the most striking of all these episodes occurred in the Sholto affair. The all-important capture of Jonathan Small, the recovery of the treasure-box and the death of the wicked Tonga (the "unhallowed dwarf with his hideous face", which in Watson's view was "enough to give a man a sleepless night") were events still to come. Yet Holmes insisted that Inspector Athelney Jones should join the two friends in a dinner at Baker Street of "oysters and a brace of grouse, with something a little choice in white wines". The meal understandably became "a merry one" as it progressed, and concluded with glasses of port all round.[3]

What was the motive behind the deceiving of Watson? In an earlier book I have shown that Holmes undoubtedly misled

---

[1] *The Veiled Lodger*, S., p. 1294.
[2] *The Missing Three-Quarter*, S., pp. 811 and 824.
[3] *The Sign of Four*, L., pp. 226–7 and 235. Mr. Earle F. Walbridge has suggested (221B. *Studies in Sherlock Holmes*, p. 56) that Holmes had a secret weakness for oysters, and that this was why he babbled of them after what Mr. Walbridge, unacquainted with the results of the present investigation, believed to have been a three-day fast. (*The Dying Detective*, S., p. 1007.) I think that there may be some truth in the same writer's belief that over-indulgence in oysters was one of the "occasional indiscretions" that led to Holmes's breakdown in health. (*The Devil's Foot*, S., p. 1041.)

Watson in regard to his attitude towards sex, and that the great detective was in fact experienced in the arts of love and thoroughly familiar with feminine psychology.[1] The object was unquestionably the gratification of Holmes's innocent vanity on the subject of his intellectual powers. He told Watson:

> "Love is an emotional thing, and whatever is emotional is opposed to that true, cold reason which I place above all things. I should never marry myself, lest I bias my judgment."[2]

Despite the evidence to the contrary, Watson was convinced:

> "[Holmes] was, I take it, the most perfect reasoning and observing machine that the world has seen: but, as a lover, he would have placed himself in a false position. He never spoke of the softer passions, save with a gibe and a sneer . . . Grit in a sensitive instrument, or a crack in one of his own high-power lenses, would not be more disturbing than a strong emotion in a nature such as his."[3]

It seems to me that there is a perfect parallel between Holmes's persuasion of Watson that he had to deny himself women if his unequalled mental powers were to be unimpaired, and his convincing of his friend that going without food was equally necessary for the same reason. The essential façade that Holmes's justifiable pride in his intellectual capacity compelled him to maintain, has already been quoted:

> "I am a brain, Watson. The rest of me is a mere appendix. Therefore, it is the brain I must consider."[4]

Holmes was not a conceited man in the accepted sense. He quite properly believed in his own ability, and told Watson that "all things should be seen exactly as they are, and to under-estimate oneself is as much a departure from truth as to exaggerate one's own powers".[5] He was convinced that he was "the last and highest court of appeal in detection",[6] and that "no man lives or has ever lived who has brought the same amount of study and of natural talent to the detection of crime which I

---

[1] "The Love Life of Sherlock Holmes", Hall, pp. 132–47.
[2] *The Sign of Four*, L., p. 270.  [3] *A Scandal in Bohemia*, S., p. 3.
[4] *The Mazarin Stone*, S., p. 1143.  [5] *The Greek Interpreter*, S., p. 479.
[6] *The Sign of Four*, L., p. 145.

have done".[1] He knew, moreover, that the impression he made upon Watson was the impression he hoped to record for posterity, for he was speaking to his biographer. "I am lost without my Boswell."[2] He doubtless felt that any picturesque emphasis he could place upon the ingredient in his personality that he considered to be of paramount importance was justifiable, even if some small deception of the gullible Watson was involved. "Logic is rare. Therefore it is upon the logic . . . that you should dwell."[3] In the records, human weakness must be suppressed and intellectual power emphasised. He did not hesitate to admonish Watson over this matter of priorities in the latter's earliest published account, *A Study in Scarlet*:

> "Detection is, or ought to be, an exact science, and should be treated in the same cold and unemotional manner. You have attempted to tinge it with romanticism."[4]

So the motive is clear. Watson was not to be allowed to make the same mistake again. What is also unfortunately clear is that whilst Holmes seems to have been capable of convincing Watson that black was white, the reader of Watson's accounts, not at close quarters with the formidable and persuasive personality of the great detective, is able to look objectively at Watson's record of the facts. Just as Watson's story of Holmes tempestuous and highly successful wooing of the maid Agatha[5] revealed the truth regarding Holmes's sexual prowess and experience, so Watson innocently and repeatedly showed that to go without food at any time was abhorrent to a man with the healthy appetite of his friend:

> "[Holmes] walked up to the sideboard, and, tearing a piece from the loaf, he devoured it voraciously, washing it down with a long draught of water.
> 'You are hungry', I remarked."[6]

And in another place:

> "He cut a slice of beef from the joint upon the sideboard, sandwiched it between two rounds of bread, and, thrusting

[1] *A Study in Scarlet*, L., pp. 23–4.     [2] *A Scandal in Bohemia*, S., p. 8.
[3] *The Copper Beeches*, S., p. 276.     [4] *The Sign of Four*, L., p. 145.
[5] *Charles Augustus Milverton*, S., pp. 726–7 and Hall, pp. 141–3.
[6] *The Five Orange Pips*, S., p. 121.

this rude meal into his pocket, he started off upon his expedition."[1]

In the compass of a single case Holmes, "springing to his feet", could not conceal from Watson his anxiety to get home to breakfast,[2] nor to delay dinner any longer:

"By Jove! my dear fellow, it is nearly nine, and the landlady babbled of green peas at seven-thirty. What with your eternal tobacco, Watson, and your irregularity at meals, I expect that you will get notice to quit, and that I shall share in your downfall."[3]

It is exceedingly surprising that in yet another case Watson did not notice that Holmes was sufficiently anxious to make sure that a large and appetising meal would await the two friends in London that he thought the matter worth the expense of a cable from Montpelier.[4] Indeed, he was so obsessed by the thought of English food that he omitted to say in the cable, in striking contrast with his usual "extreme exactness and astuteness",[5] whether Mrs. Hudson was to prepare at an early hour one of her unequalled breakfasts or an epicurean dinner in the evening:

"Now, Watson, if you will pack your bag I will cable to Mrs. Hudson to make one of her best efforts for two hungry travellers at seven-thirty tomorrow."[6]

I must concede that for me to suggest that Holmes used his great ability as an actor[7] to cover up both inconsistency and the actual deceiving of Watson is a serious business indeed. I would naturally refrain from such a comment if the absolute proof was not available in the text. As to the lack of consistency,

---

[1] *The Beryl Coronet*, S., p. 266.   [2] *The Three Students*, S., p. 782.
[3] *Ibid.*, p. 776.
[4] I have been subjected to friendly criticism by laymen for copying this spelling of the French town of Montpellier from *The Empty House*, S., p. 569, in my earlier book (p. 112). I do so again with fearless obstinacy, this time copying from the text of *Lady Frances Carfax*, S., pp. 1021 and 1024, in the fullest confidence that every Sherlockian will applaud my choice of my authority.
[5] *The Red-Headed League*, S., p. 45.
[6] *Lady Frances Carfax*, S., p. 1027. The case was less than half-way completed when the cable was sent.
[7] This talent is fully discussed and documented on p. 29 of my previous book, and see also *The Sign of Four*, L., p. 225. " 'Ah, you rogue!' cried Jones, highly delighted. 'You would have made an actor, and a rare one. You had the proper workhouse cough, and those weak legs of yours are worth ten pounds a week.' "

what could be more at variance, for example, than Holmes's words about the effect of smoking on the appetite in the case of "the professor, it was she" on the one hand, compared with what he did in the affair of Mr. Victor Hatherley, the hydraulic engineer? In the first example, Holmes asked the housekeeper at Yoxley Old Place, "the good Mrs. Marker", about Professor Coram's excessive consumption of cigarettes:

" 'His health—well, I don't know that it's better nor worse for the smoking.'
'Ah!' said Holmes, 'but it kills the appetite.' "[1]

We are entitled to be severely critical of the sincerity of this observation, when we recall the scene that met Watson and Hatherley when they arrived at Baker Street early one morning:

"Sherlock Holmes was, as I expected, lounging about his sitting-room in his dressing-gown, reading the agony column of *The Times*, and smoking his before-breakfast pipe, which was composed of all the plugs and dottles left from his smokes of the day before, all carefully dried and collected on the corner of the mantelpiece. He received us in his quietly genial fashion, ordered fresh rashers and eggs, and joined us in a hearty meal."[2]

For the melancholy proof of Holmes's actual deceit in regard to his alleged austerity over food whilst working on a case we need no further documentary evidence than two passages from the text of *The Hound of the Baskervilles*. It will be recalled that Watson discovered to his extreme surprise that despite his belief that his friend was in London, Holmes was secretly camping out in one of the neolithic stone dwellings on the lonely moor surrounding Baskerville Hall. Watson had asked how Holmes was managing for food in these conditions, and was told:

---

[1] *The Golden Pince-Nez*, S., pp. 799–800.
[2] *The Engineer's Thumb*, S., p. 205. Friends whose opinion I value tell me that the mere recital of the revolting contents of Holmes's "before-breakfast pipe" is sufficient to cause any person with a sensitive stomach to recoil from the thought of food. In parenthesis, one wonders a little about the ordering of "fresh rashers and eggs". Was the hearty meal Holmes enjoyed with Watson and Hatherley conceivably his *second* breakfast that morning?

"I brought Cartwright down with me—you remember the little chap at the Express office—and he has seen after my simple wants: a loaf of bread and a clean collar. What does man want more?"

What indeed? Watson's inspection of the interior of the hut revealed a good deal more than a loaf of bread. We must presume that only the demands of friendship and the dominating personality of the great detective prevented Watson from succumbing to the extreme temptation of answering Holmes's question with a simple statement of the facts. In the hut was "a pannikin and a half-full bottle of spirits" and "a loaf of bread, a tinned tongue, and two tins of preserved peaches". Watson noticed, too, "a litter of empty tins", but did not record for our interest what choice selection of delicacies they had doubtless contained.[1]

It must be said in Holmes's favour that he made an exceedingly frank remark during the earliest days of his association with his biographer, that should have put Watson on his guard. Holmes correctly prophesied that Inspectors Gregson and Lestrade would obtain all the credit for the solving of the Jefferson Hope case, a forecast which the innocent Watson had difficulty in accepting:

" 'I don't see that they had very much to do with his capture,' I answered.

'What you do in this world is a matter of no consequence', returned my companion bitterly. 'The question is, what can you make people believe that you have done.' "[2]

[1] *The Hound of the Baskervilles*, L., pp. 402 and 406.
[2] *A Study in Scarlet*, L., p. 133.

PLATE I. Holmes wearing his deerstalker, or
"earflapped travelling cap"(?).
(*see p.* 4)

PLATE II. Holmes and Watson interrupted at one of Mrs.
Hudson's breakfasts by the arrival of Mr. John Hector
McFarlane (*see pp.* 13 and 125)

# II

# THE BOOK-COLLECTOR

IN 1953 Miss Madeleine B. Stern, a distinguished New York antiquarian book-seller and a Sherlockian scholar well known on both sides of the Atlantic, published a long essay demonstrating her belief that Sherlock Holmes was one of the great book-collectors of the nineteenth and early twentieth centuries.[1] He was, Miss Stern asserted, "an avid book collector"[2] who was "able and eager to acquire a fine collection of rarities".[3] She said that the new acquisitions which he regularly added to "his many fine books"[4] following his frequent "visits to the rare and secondhand bookshops of London"[5] (and especially those in the Strand "where books towered to the ceiling and spilled over on to the floors as Holmes browsed among them"[6]) unquestionably "joined shelves already resplendent with the calf and vellum bound volumes that definitely bore a Holmes ownership inscription".[7] Every item Holmes owned, wrote Miss Stern, "was almost always a worthy book, and it was almost always in a rare or first edition".[8] These pronouncements by an acknowledged authority are worthy of our closest attention.

We know, of course, that Holmes was already interested in books when still an undergraduate of twenty-one at Trinity College, Cambridge, for he told Watson that one of the attractions of his holiday in 1873 at Donnithorpe, the Norfolk country home of "Justice of the Peace Trevor", was the "small

---

[1] "Sherlock Holmes: Rare-Book Collector. A Study in Book Detection", *The Papers of the Bibliographical Society of America*, New York, 1953, xlvii, pp. 133-55.
[2] *Ibid.*, p. 149.  [3] *Ibid.*, p. 155.  [4] *Ibid.*, p. 153.
[5] *Ibid.*, p. 155.  [6] *Ibid.*, p. 154.  [7] *Ibid.*, p. 145.
[8] *Ibid.*, p. 145.

but select library, taken over, as I understand, from a former occupant".[1] It may, indeed, be significant that his unvoiced criticism of his host was that he was "a man of little culture . . . He knew hardly any books".[2] We know too, that Holmes's concern with books was life-long, for during Watson's account of the last case in which the two friends were involved he remarked:

"But you had retired, Holmes. We heard of you living the life of a hermit among your bees and your books in a small farm upon the South Downs."[3]

Watson recorded that when he admonished Holmes in regard to his drug habit, the great detective "raised his eyes languidly from the old black-letter volume which he had opened".[4] Watson said that after his marriage to Mary Morstan he saw little of Holmes, who "remained in our lodgings in Baker Street, buried among his old books".[5] It cannot be disputed, therefore, that Holmes was a book owner for most of his life and that some of the volumes he possessed were undoubtedly old. Whether these facts justify Miss Stern's estimate of him as an active and distinguished book-collector, however, is a matter upon which I have some reservations.

It is noteworthy in this connexion, perhaps, that the name of Sherlock Holmes is mentioned neither by Seymour de Ricci[6] nor John Carter[7] in their histories of book collecting. It must be conceded, however, that since neither of these authorities had anything to tell us about the Hon. George Richard Nassau (1756–1823), for example, this negative evidence is inconclusive. Nassau, who was the High Sheriff of Suffolk and the brother of the fifth Earl of Rochford, had "long held a distinguished rank among the collectors of rare and curious books".[8] His great library of emblem books, early English poetry, the drama, rare old books on conjuring and above all on the topography and history of his native county of Suffolk, was

---

[1] *The "Gloria Scott"*, S., p. 376.
[2] *Ibid.*, p. 376.
[3] *His Last Bow*, S., p. 1082.
[4] *The Sign of Four*, L., p. 144.
[5] *A Scandal in Bohemia*, S., p. 4.
[6] *English Collectors of Books and Manuscripts* (Cambridge, 1930).
[7] *Taste & Technique in Book-Collecting* (Cambridge, 1948).
[8] *The Gentleman's Magazine and Historical Chronicle* (London, 1823, xciii, Part 2) pp. 178–9.

sold by auction by the London bookseller, Robert Harding Evans, in two sections in February and March, 1824.[1] The sale contained 4,264 lots and realised the large sum (in those days) of £8,500. Nassau's remarkable career as a collector was described by Nichols,[2] and an account of his library was recorded by Clarke.[3] It can therefore be argued, I suppose, that since Nassau's name does not appear in either of precisely the two popular treatises on book-collecting where we might have expected to find it, the similar omission of Sherlock Holmes is not significant.

It will be seen that I have done my best for Miss Stern in this regard by pointing to a comparable omission by both de Ricci and Carter, but I fear that I cannot assist her in the similar and doubly unfortunate failure of W. Carew Hazlitt to pay any tribute to Sherlock Holmes as a book-collector. The twelfth part of *Contributions towards a Dictionary of English Book-Collectors, and also of some Foreign Collectors whose Libraries were incorporated in English Collections* (14 parts, London 1892–1912), edited by Bernard Quaritch, was "An Alphabetical Roll Call of Book Collectors from 1316 to 1898, by W. C. Hazlitt". The name of Sherlock Holmes, regrettably from Miss Stern's point of view, was omitted from both this work and from Hazlitt's much larger *A Roll of Honour. A Calendar of the Names of over* 17,000 *Men and Women who throughout the British Isles and in our Early Colonies have collected MSS. and Printed Books from the XIVth to the XIXth Century . . . To which are added indexes of localities, and of ranks and occupations* (London, 1908).

Miss Stern is obviously of the convinced opinion that Holmes was possessed of considerable technical expertise in his approach to his avocation. She tells us that he was "an expert book collector"[4] ("an expert in book collection",[5] indeed) and that he used "his expert eye [when] glancing at a calf or vellum back".[6] Miss Stern does not quote her authority for these assertions,

---

[1] *List of Catalogues of English Sales*, 1676–1900, *now in the British Museum* (London, 1915), p. 157.
[2] J. and J. B. Nichols, *Illustrations of the Literary History of the Eighteenth Century* (8 vols., London, 1817–58) vi, pp. 327–43.
[3] W. Clarke, *Repertorium Bibliographicum* (London, 1819), p. 398.
[4] Stern, *op. cit.*, p. 151.     Stern, *op. cit.*, p. 153.     [6] Stern, *op. cit.*, p. 154.

and we must assume, therefore, that they are based, perhaps with more enthusiasm than justification, upon two passages in the canon. The first occurred in a remark by Holmes to Mrs. Maberley in regard to the very curious offer to buy her house and the whole of its contents, made on behalf of Isadora Klein/Persano, an unusual person of whom I shall have something to say in another context later in this book. The contract was in such all-embracing and yet definite terms that Mrs. Maberley's solicitor had advised her that if she signed it she would not be able to remove even her private possessions. Holmes said:

" 'There are always some lunatics about. It would be a dull world without them. At first I thought of some buried valuable. But why, in that case, should they want your furniture? You don't happen to have a Raphael or a First Folio Shakespeare without knowing it?'

'No, I don't think I have anything rarer than a Crown Derby tea-set.' "[1]

The second suggested that Holmes knew a leaf from an octavo when he saw one, and that he was aware of the existence and importance of watermarks. He was commenting upon a letter (notably lacking in physical attraction) received by Mrs. Neville St. Clair:

"Written in pencil upon a fly-leaf of a book, octavo size, no watermark. Posted today in Gravesend by a man with a dirty thumb. Ha! And the flap has been gummed, if I am not very much in error, by a person who had been chewing tobacco."[2]

Miss Stern makes it clear that in her opinion Holmes's collection of rare books was a large one. She deduces that there were "philosophical and agricultural shelves"[3] and at least one "medico-criminal bookshelf".[4] She asserts that "law, philosophy literature, natural history, philology—all are represented by the rare books or first editions definitely known to have belonged to Holmes. For him, no overspecialized collecting".[5] The latter phrase is significant. It is the basic assumption upon which

---

[1] *The Three Gables*, S., pp. 1165–6.
[2] *The Man with the Twisted Lip*, S., p. 140.
[3] Stern, *op. cit.*, p. 153.   [4] Stern, *op. cit.*, p. 152.   [5] Stern, *op. cit.*, p. 141.

Miss Stern relies for her deduction that Holmes must have owned many rare books, for she refers repeatedly to "the broadness of his interests",[1] his "catholicity of interest"[2] and her belief that "his interests were many and generalized".[3] This premise that Holmes's library was large is, of course, one upon which Miss Stern must of necessity insist if her argument that Holmes was one of the great book-collectors is to stand up.

Holbrook Jackson, writing of book collections, said "What their size should be, how many books, invites many opinions",[4] but he left it in no doubt that a true collector's accumulation of rare volumes would be substantial. Bibliomaniacs like George III owned 60,000 books, whilst Richard Heber possessed five libraries. Let us be fair to Miss Stern, however, and employ the minimum standards of measurement to the necessary number of books Holmes must have owned to justify any claim that he was a great collector. Mark Pattison laid down the precept that "no man could respect himself unless he possessed at least 1000 volumes",[5] and this seems to me to be confirmed by the size of the "cabinet collections" of Montaigne and Locker-Lampson, whose deliberate restraint and connoisseurship confined their libraries respectively to 1000 and 1247 books. Let us assume, therefore, that Miss Stern invites us to believe that Holmes owned no more than this number, as we address ourselves to the interesting problem of how Holmes managed to accommodate them.

Miss Stern tells us that Holmes's rare books were on "shelves in the treasure room of Baker Street".[6] We are in serious difficulty at once when we recall Watson's quite precise description of No. 221B:

"We met next day as he had arranged, and inspected the rooms at No. 221B, Baker Street, of which he had spoken at our meeting. They consisted of a couple of comfortable bedrooms and a single large airy sitting-room, cheerfully furnished, and illuminated by two broad windows."[7]

Holmes obviously had no space at all for bookshelves in his bedroom, for that was occupied by the immense wardrobes

---

[1] Stern, *op. cit.*, p. 148.  [2] Stern, *op. cit.*, p. 149.  [3] Stern, *op. cit.*, p. 149.
[4] *The Anatomy of Bibliomania* (New Edition, London, 1950), p. 339.
[5] *Ibid.*, p. 339.  [6] Stern, *op. cit.*, p. 155.  [7] *A Study in Scarlet*, L., p. 14.

filled to bursting-point with his innumerable disguises, to which I shall have occasion to refer later. The sitting-room was large, but we have to remember that it was also the dining-room, containing a table (complete with chairs) at which at least five people could sit,[1] a sofa,[2] several easy chairs and Holmes's desk.[3] A complete corner of the room was occupied by the "acid-stained deal-topped table"[4] on which stood Holmes's very considerable chemical paraphernalia, including "retorts"[5] and "a formidable array of bottles and test tubes".[6] In parenthesis, there was also Watson's bull pup, but it may be argued (properly, I think) that this animal was completely unobtrusive, being mentioned on only one occasion during the entire canon,[7] and would therefore only minimally affect the situation.

The fact that space in the sitting-room was extremely limited is additionally proved, if further proof be necessary, by the fact that Holmes had to keep "his cigars in the coal-scuttle, his tobacco in the toe-end of a Persian slipper, and his unanswered correspondence transfixed by a jack-knife into the very centre of his wooden mantelpiece".[8] It may be thought, moreover, that whatever bookshelves there were would be filled to capacity by other than collector's items.[9] They would surely be groaning under the weight of the twenty-six "great index volume[s]" of Holmes's homemade encyclopaedia[10] and the "row of for-

---

[1] *The Noble Bachelor*, S., p. 240. It may be urged that only Mr. and Mrs. Francis Hay Moulton joined Holmes and Watson in the "quite epicurean little cold supper" at Baker Street. We must remember, however, that Lord Robert St. Simon was invited to join in the "friendly supper", but asked to be excused. "I may be forced to acquiesce in these recent developments, but I can hardly be expected to make merry over them." (*Ibid.*, pp. 245–6).

[2] *A Study in Scarlet*, L., p. 14, and *The Musgrave Ritual*, S., p. 397. During the acutely lethargic periods of his manic-depression, Holmes "would lie upon the sofa in the sitting-room, hardly uttering a word or moving a muscle from morning to night".

[3] *The Dancing Men*, S., p. 611.      [4] *The Empty House*, S., p. 578.
[5] *The Sign of Four*, L., p. 219.      [6] *A Case of Identity*, S., p. 69.
[7] *A Study in Scarlet*, L., p. 13.      [8] *The Musgrave Ritual*, S., p. 396.

[9] This is supported by Watson's remark that "every corner of the room was stacked with bundles of manuscript" (*The Musgrave Ritual*, S., p. 397) for which there was clearly no room anywhere else. Watson was guilty here of a slight overstatement, in that we know that one corner was entirely and permanently occupied by Holmes's apparatus for his chemical experiments, but the argument is only marginally affected.

[10] *The Sussex Vampire*, S., p. 1179. These "huge books" are also described in *The Veiled Lodger*, S., p. 1291. They would, of course, be unique and priceless collector's items today, but it is proper to assume that Holmes would not regard them in that light.

midable scrap-books and books of reference which many of our fellow-citizens would have been so glad to burn".[1] Miss Stern's case is not helped, moreover, by the fact that clearly no attempt had been made to line all the sitting-room walls with shelving to house the supposed rare book collection. We have positive proof in the text that one wall, at least, was kept entirely clear to enable Holmes to indulge in another expensive hobby, involving noise, general inconvenience and frequent replastering and redecoration:

> "Holmes in one of his queer humours would sit in an arm-chair, with his hair-trigger and a hundred Boxer cartridges, and proceed to adorn the opposite wall with a patriotic V.R. done in bullet-pocks."[2]

With the facts of the matter established we can now see that Miss Stern's attractive hypothesis of "the treasure room of Baker Street"[3] and the "shelves of 221B"[4] will not do. On the other hand, I think that it would be unfair to dismiss the main theme of Miss Stern's agreeable dissertation, that Holmes was a great book-collector, merely because part of it has broken down under scrutiny. Indeed, if another of Miss Stern's minor assertions is considered and the proper inference made, her main contention becomes rather more credible. I refer to her belief that Holmes was "canny and secretive in his book collecting practices"[5] and that "even from Watson, however, Holmes successfully concealed the nature and extent of his bibliographical rarities".[6] Miss Stern tells us without ambiguity that his collection was "a secret hoard of rare books"[7] and that "he would find his treasures and enjoy them in solitude. Bibliographically, he would walk alone."[8]

If Miss Stern believes this, then it is hard to understand why

---

[1] *The Empty House*, S., p. 578. The works of reference were clearly numerous (Watson described them as "a line of books of reference" in *The Noble Bachelor*, S., p. 226) and included, among many others, *Crockford's Clerical Directory* (*The Retired Colourman*, S., p. 1327), some sort of "Continental Gazetteer" (*A Scandal in Bohemia*, S., p. 7) *Whitaker's Almanack* for more than one year (*The Valley of Fear*, L., pp. 465–6), a "red-covered" volume of genealogy (*The Noble Bachelor*, S., p. 226) and the London Telephone Directory (*The Three Garridebs*, S., p. 1197).

[2] *The Musgrave Ritual*, S., p. 396.    [3] Stern, *op. cit.*, p. 155.
[4] Stern, *op. cit.*, p. 135.    [5] Stern, *op. cit.*, p. 133.
[6] Stern, *op. cit.*, p. 134.    [7] Stern, *op. cit.*, p. 136.    [8] Stern, *op. cit.*, p. 135.

she has even considered the possibility that the library was at
221B Baker Street. I have tried to document my conviction that
there was not room for a thousand books in that crowded sitting-
room in any event, but what is quite certain is that if by any
stretch of imagination the collection was somehow squeezed
in, its presence could not have been concealed from Watson.

I find it surprising that so diligent a Sherlockian student as
Miss Stern has not noticed a remark by Watson (admittedly
buried deeply in the canon and never repeated) which is worthy
of close examination:

> "Holmes was working somewhere under one of the numer-
> ous disguises and names with which he concealed his own
> formidable identity. He had at least five small refuges in
> different parts of London in which he was able to change his
> personality."[1]

In an earlier essay I have expressed my belief that Watson was
misled by his friend over Holmes's keen interest in food, and I
have shown in a previous work that Watson was mildly bamboozled by Holmes in regard to the latter's attitude towards
women.[2] In my view, the motive for these small deceptions lay
in the fact that Watson was the great detective's biographer
as well as his friend. Holmes was anxious, for not unworthy
reasons, that the record for posterity should be an uncomplicated
picture of himself as "the most perfect reasoning and observing
machine that the world has seen",[3] sacrificing all material
indulgences for the sake of "that true cold reason which I place
above all things".[4]

In the circumstances, it is perhaps not surprising that Watson
swallowed Holmes's explanation of the purpose for which he
maintained five small secret establishments in addition to the
rooms in Baker Street, as other commentators seem to have
done.[5] Four quotations from the many similar examples in the

---

[1] *Black Peter*, S., p. 697.　　　　　　[2] Hall, *op. cit.*, pp. 132–47.
[3] *A Scandal in Bohemia*, S., p. 3.　　[4] *The Sign of Four*, L., p. 270.
[5] The only specific observation by another commentator on this small mystery
that I have been able to find is by Vincent Starrett, who remarked that the single
mention in the canon of the "five small refuges" had generally been overlooked.
"The reference is tantalizing and obscure. The rooms of Mycroft Holmes, opposite
the Diogenes Club, would certainly be one of them; but it would be satisfying to
know the others. At such times—when he was operating in disguise—Holmes
sometimes took the name of 'Captain Basil', the better to deceive his casual

text are sufficient, however, completely to demolish the suggestion that Holmes used these unrevealed apartments in which to store his numerous disguises. They were, of course, kept in his bedroom at Baker Street:

"It was close upon four before the door opened, and a drunken-looking groom, ill-kempt and side-whiskered with an inflamed face and disreputable clothes, walked into the room. Accustomed as I was to my friend's amazing power in the use of disguises, I had to look three times before I was certain that it was indeed he. With a nod he vanished into the bedroom, whence he emerged in five minutes tweed-suited and respectable, as of old."[1]

"It was not yet three when we found ourselves in our room once more. [Holmes] hurried to his chamber, and was [out] again in a few minutes dressed as a common loafer. With his collar turned up, his shiny seedy coat, his red cravat, and his worn boots, he was a perfect sample of the class."[2]

"With the gesture of a man who has taken his decision, [Holmes] sprang to his feet and passed into his bedroom. A little later a rakish young workman with a goatee beard and a swagger lit his clay pipe at the lamp before descending into the street. 'I'll be back some time, Watson', said he, and vanished into the night."[3]

" 'He's following someone. Yesterday he was out as a workman looking for a job. Today he was an old woman. Fairly took me in, he did, and I ought to know his ways by now.' Billy pointed with a grin to a very baggy parasol which leaned against the sofa. 'That's part of the old woman's outfit', he said . . . The bedroom door opened, and the long thin form of Holmes emerged."[4]

It will be recalled that I suggested (p. 27) that all available space in Holmes's bedroom was occupied by large wardrobes, and the foregoing extracts from the text prove that it was indeed in his bedroom at Baker Street that the detective kept his

assistants and to deceive and confound his unsuspecting enemies. It may be assumed that in all of his five refuges he stored the materials of deception, as well as quantities of shag tobacco." (Starrett, p. 83.)

[1] *A Scandal in Bohemia*, S., p. 14.  [2] *The Beryl Coronet*, S., p. 266.
[3] *Charles Augustus Milverton*, S., p. 726.
[4] *The Mazarin Stone*, S., pp. 1141-2.

"numerous disguises" and "was able to change his personality". It follows that the "five small refuges in different parts of London"[1] were maintained for a quite different purpose. I find it surprising that Miss Stern has not claimed that it was obviously in these hidden apartments, and not at Baker Street at all, that Holmes kept his "secret hoard of rare books"[2] which he "successfully concealed" even from Watson.[3] She could persuasively have argued that it would have been entirely typical of Holmes's sense of the appropriate to have followed, in perfect miniature, the pattern set by the great collector Richard Heber, who owned five libraries and kept them in separate houses in England and on the Continent.[4] Another example that Miss Stern might have suggested would have been attractive to Holmes was that of Richard de Bury, who had separate stores of rare books "at his manor-houses and at his palace at Auckland. The floor of his hall was so strewn with manuscripts that it was hard to reach his presence."[5] She could have claimed a peculiar significance for the latter sentence, when we recall the bundles of manuscript stacked in every corner of the sitting-room at Baker Street.

Miss Stern could, I think, profitably have supported her opinion that Holmes was a great book-collector if she had quoted a sentence by John Carter:

> "There is undoubtedly a greater tendency for book-collecting to flourish in persons of studious or reflective temper than among pugilists or aviators; and certain professions, like surgery and the law, seem especially favoured to it."[6]

Perhaps she refrained from so doing because of Holmes's undoubted skill at fisticuffs:

> "Not Mr. Sherlock Holmes!" roared the prize-fighter. 'God's truth! How could I have mistook you? If instead o' standin' there so quiet you had just stepped up and given me that cross-hit of yours under the jaw, I'd ha' known

---

[1] *Black Peter*, S., p. 697.    [2] Stern, *op. cit.*, p. 134.    [3] Stern, *op. cit.*, p. 136.
[4] *The Anatomy of Bibliomania* op. cit., p. 339, *Taste & Technique in Book-Collecting*, op. cit., p. 15 and *English Collectors of Books and Manuscripts*, op. cit., p. 102.
[5] *The Anatomy of Bibliomania*, op. cit., p. 344.
[6] *Taste & Technique in Book-Collecting*, op. cit., p. 2.

you without a question. Ah, you're one that has wasted your gifts, you have!' "[1]

This apart, I think that the weight of Carter's observation is generally in her favour, for we know that Holmes was "a man of studious and quiet habits",[2] that his knowledge of anatomy was accurate if unsystematic[3] and that he had "a good practical knowledge of British law."[4]

I hope that it may be thought that I have been fair to Miss Stern in my epitome of her submission, and that she will pardon my temerity in having offered one or two suggestions as to how her argument could perhaps have been strengthened here and there in matters of small detail. This is a natural preamble to my saying, with regret, that I find myself in amiable disagreement with the whole of her conclusions.

Book-collectors are not merely accumulators. Magpies, it has been pointed out, have an acquisitive instinct, and a similarly indiscriminate passion for accumulating junk afflicts one in a hundred of the human race. One wonders, a little uneasily in this context, about those "bundles of manuscript which were on no account to be burned" and Holmes's "horror of destroying documents".[5] There is a distinction too, between collectors and the formers of libraries. Holmes unquestionably gathered about him many books of reference that he needed in the course of his work, and we can do nothing but admire his diligence and expertise in constructing his own great encyclopedia when he discovered that those available in print were not adequate for his purpose.[6] Worthy of praise though all this was, it did not, of course, qualify Holmes as a collector. A. W. Pollard defined book-collecting as "the bringing together of books which in their contents, their form or the history of the individual copy possess some element of permanent interest, and either actually or prospectively are rare, in the sense of being difficult to

---

[1] *The Sign of Four*, L., p. 176. These authoritative comments came from a Mr. McMurdo, well-known in the prize-ring prior to his retirement and benefit match in 1884, when Holmes and he fought three exhibition rounds at Alison's rooms.
[2] *A Study in Scarlet*, L., p. 8.     [3] *Ibid.*, p. 18.     [4] *Ibid.*, p. 18.
[5] *The Musgrave Ritual*, S., pp. 396–7.
[6] It must be said, however, that his method of indexing was unusual. His entries under "V" of "Voyage of the *Gloria Scott*, "Victor Lynch, the forger" and "Venomous lizard", for example, cannot have been initially helpful to the researcher seeking information on these subjects (*The Sussex Vampire*, S., p. 1179.)

procure".[1] It is therefore the evidence for Holmes's interest in rare books that we must presently examine.

It is not in dispute that the books forming a true collection will possess a common factor, whether it be author, subject,[2] binding, date or even place of publication:

> "The quality of such a collection lies in the fact that the coherent whole will be infinitely greater than the mere sum of the separate parts: its value is a cumulative one, and each book in it, by being related to its neighbours, both receives from them and gives to them an added lustre."[3]

In another place, Carter said of the collector:

> "He is rather a man . . . who has a reverence for and a desire to possess, the original or some other specifically admirable, curious or interesting edition of a book he loves or respects or one which has a special place among his intellectual interests. Furthermore, he enjoys, with a degree of intensity which will vary according to his temperament, his training and the standards of his fellow-bibliophiles, that exercise of his natural and intellectual faculties which is involved in the application of knowledge, observation, ingenuity, foresight, enterprise and persistence to the pursuit of his quarry, its scrutiny and appraisal when found, its use and perhaps formal description when secured."[4]

With these observations to guide us, we can now turn to the very few references in the text of the canon that are relevant and decide whether Holmes was a great book-collector or not. Miss Stern attaches great importance to the first of these, part of a conversation between Holmes and Watson at Baker Street:

> " 'This is a queer old book I picked up at a stall yesterday —*De Jure inter Gentes*—published in Latin at Liège in the Lowlands, in 1642. Charles's head was still firm on his shoulders when this little brown-backed volume was struck off.'
> 'Who is the printer?'

---

[1] "Book-Collecting", *Encyclopaedia Britannica*, 11th Edition.

[2] It is pleasant to record that John Carter ( *Taste & Technique in Book-Collecting*, op. cit., p. 7) cited *Sherlock Holmes* as one of his three examples of a subject-collection.

[3] *New Paths in Book-Collecting* (London, 1934), p. 4.

[4] *Taste & Technique in Book-Collecting*, op. cit., pp. 9–10.

'Phillipe de Croy, whoever he may have been. On the
fly-leaf, in very faded ink, is written 'Ex Libris Guliemi
Whyte'. I wonder who William Whyte was. Some prag-
matical seventeenth-century lawyer, I suppose.' "[1]

According to all other published bibliographical information
*Juris et Judicii fecialis, sive, Juris inter gentes,*[2] by Richard Zouche
(1590–1661), was first published as a quarto at Oxford in
1650.[3] One year later the book was published at Leyden, with a
title closely approximating to that of the edition owned by
Holmes, and another edition printed in Oxford appeared in
1658.[4] All three are very considerable prizes in any collection
of rare legal books. Holmes's find, however, was of supreme
importance, pre-dating as it did by eight years the edition that
had been universally accepted as the *editio princeps.*[5] The Liège
edition of 1642 was so completely unknown that it is not listed
in Xavier de Theux de Montjardin's *Bibliographie Liègoise,
contenant* 1°. *Les Livres imprimés a Liège depuis le XVI<sup>e</sup> siècle.*
2°. *Les ouvrages publiés . . . concernant l'histoire de l'ancienne
principauté de Liège* (2 pts., Bruxelles, 1867), nor in the
*Deuxième édition augmentée* of the same work, published in
Bruges in 1885. In these circumstances, it may be thought that
Holmes's assessment of it merely as "a queer old book" was
conspicuously uninformed.

The sometime owner of this extremely rare and probably
unique item was William White (1604–78) the distinguished
English writer and divine, a fact of which Holmes was evidently
unaware. We may think, therefore, that Miss Stern's argument,
on which she relies throughout her essay, that "it is certainly
not too much to assume that the man who captured the 1642

[1] *A Study in Scarlet*, L., p. 48.
[2] According to Wing (iii, Z20) there are copies in the libraries of the Universi-
ties of Oxford, Cambridge and Yale, Trinity College, Dublin, those of the Royal
College of Physicians, Harvard Law School and the Union Theological Seminary of
New York, the National Library of Scotland and the William A. Clark Library of
Los Angeles. The copy once owned by the British Museum was destroyed by
enemy action in the 1939–45 War. Like many other missing books, however, it is
still listed in the Catalogue (6955.b.52.) without comment.
[3] The imprint reads, "Oxoniae, excudebat H. Hall, impensis Tho. Robinson."
[4] Wing, iii, Z21.
[5] It is noteworthy that when the Oxford edition of 1650 was re-published in
two volumes in 1911, edited by Thomas Erskine Holland, it was firmly described
"A reproduction of the first edition (1650)".

Zouche continued to add treasures of equal stature to his collection"[1] is not convincing.

It has been said that in book-collecting it is not the early bird that catches the worm, but the bird that knows a worm when he sees one. The available evidence unfortunately suggests that Holmes did not know that Zouche was the author of the "queer old book" of which he was the owner, and that the astounding date of the imprint had no significance for him. The name of the printer was dismissed in an aside, "whoever he may have been", which smacked of indifference. His careless reference to the previous owner (which was incorrect so far as it went) suggested rather plainly that he was unlikely to take the trouble to obtain any information about him. The binding was presumably in calf, and may or may not have been original, but Holmes was not informative on the point. So far as he was concerned, his book was "brown-backed" and that was sufficient for him. It must be said, with all respect for the opposite view taken by Miss Stern, that these are not the attitudes we would expect of a true collector.

It will be recalled that when Holmes returned to London from the dead (or rather, from the Reichenbach) in 1894, causing Watson to faint "for the first and the last time in my life",[2] the detective first appeared to his friend disguised as an aged bookseller, claiming to be the proprietor of a "little bookshop at the corner of Church Street".[3] As all this was a deception Miss Stern considers (I think rightly) that the books that the disguised Holmes playfully tried to sell to Watson, before the latter collapsed and had to be restored with brandy, must have come from the detective's own shelves:

> "Maybe you collect yourself, sir; here's *British Birds*, and *Catullus*, and *The Holy War*—a bargain every one of them. With five volumes you could just fill that gap on that second shelf. It looks untidy, does it not, sir?"[4]

To these three items belonging to Holmes Miss Stern properly adds another, the title of which Watson had noticed during his

---

[1] Stern, *op. cit.*, p. 135.   [2] *The Empty House*, S., p. 564.   [3] *Ibid.*, p. 564.
[4] *Ibid.*, p. 564. The "five volumes" are accounted for if it is assumed that *The Origin of Tree Worship* was included, and that *British Birds* was the Newcastle edition in two volumes, as Miss Stern suggests.

earlier encounter with the pseudo-book-seller in Park Lane, when the latter had dropped all the books he was carrying on to the pavement:

"I remember that as I picked them up I observed the title of one of them, *The Origin of Tree Worship.*"[1]

Miss Stern identifies these four books respectively as "the fine *History of British Birds* with the Bewick wood engravings printed in two volumes at Newcastle in 1797 and 1804",[2] "the first Aldine Catullus: *Catullus Tibullus. Propertius,* printed in italic letter by Aldus at Venice in 1502",[3] "a copy of the 1639 first edition of Thomas Fuller's *Historie of the Holy Warre*"[4] and "*Der Baumkultus,* written by Boetticher in 1856, a title which Watson, for the sake of his English public, translated a bit too freely".[5]

If Miss Stern is right, these volumes were, without exception, rare and valuable items. A proper inference is that Holmes did not know that they were (it is reasonable to recall here the precedent of his lamentable ignorance of the importance of his priceless 1642 Zouche) and because of this lack of knowledge he attached but scant value to them. If this were not so, it seems obvious that in the uncertainty of the English weather he would not have risked carrying them under his arm in Park Lane, as he did, without even the crude protection of a piece of brown paper around them. He would not have contemplated for one moment the hazard of dropping them in the dirt (which in the event occurred) nor of having them snatched from him, by conveying them in this careless fashion through a busy London street infested by "loafers upon the pavements".[6]

There is another thing. If Holmes had really been a serious collector he would have been well acquainted with a number of antiquarian booksellers and their method of approach to a prospective customer. Holmes was a master of disguise and an accomplished actor. Watson said of him:

[1] *The Empty House,* S., p. 563.   [2] Stern, *op. cit.,* p. 139.   [3] Stern, *op. cit.,* p. 138.
[4] Stern, *op. cit.,* p. 139. This identification seems improbable. The four seventeenth-century editions of Fuller's *Historie* were all large and heavy folios, which Holmes would be unlikely to choose to carry under his arm. Miss Stern seems to have overlooked the near certainty, for reasons of size and exactness of title, that the book was John Bunyan's *The Holy War,* first published in 1682.
[5] Stern, *op. cit.,* p. 139.   [6] *The Empty House,* S., p. 562.

"It was not merely that Holmes changed his costume. His expression, his manner, his very soul seemed to vary with every fresh part that he assumed. The stage lost a fine actor, even as science lost an acute reasoner, when he became a specialist in crime."[1]

With all this accepted, can we believe for one moment that if Holmes had known anything whatever of the antiquarian book trade, his simulation of a member of that honourable profession offering to a customer four superb items (worth a considerable sum of money even in 1894) would have been on the mundane basis that they would "just fill that gap on that second shelf"?[2]

As I have had occasion to say earlier in another context, it will not do. These items had casually been "picked up" (the words are Holmes's) from time to time, it would seem, without any central collecting theme. The latter fact is surely demonstrated by the lack of any connexion between the authors, subjects, dates or places of publication of the items concerned. To Holmes they were simply "queer old book[s]"[3] and were presumably bought at prices that seemed "a bargain every one of them". The fact that Holmes was attracted by bargains is well illustrated by the "great exultation" with which he told Watson "how he had purchased his own Stradivarius, which was worth at least five hundred guineas, at a Jew broker's in Tottenham Court Road for fifty-five shillings".[5]

Once the solution to a mystery is in sight, all difficulties begin to disappear and everything fits into place. Now that we know that Holmes was not a collector at all, but simply a man who built up an admirable working library, and at the same time could not resist "a queer old book" if it was cheap, we begin to notice significant paragraphs in the canon that are completely inconsistent with any other conclusion. Would any collector, for example, describe his books as Holmes did to Watson?

"A man should keep his little brain attic stocked with all the furniture that he is likely to use, and the rest he can put away in the lumber-room of his library, where he can get it if he wants it."[6]

[1] *A Scandal in Bohemia*, S., p. 20.  [2] *The Empty House*, S., p. 564.
[3] *A Study in Scarlet*, L., p. 48.  [4] *The Empty House*, S., p. 564.
[5] *The Cardboard Box.*, S., p. 935.  [6] *The Five Orange Pips*, S., p. 116.

Would any collector, especially one in retirement with un-limited time to devote to his books, be content to keep them in such disorder that an hour's search was necessary to find the Rev. J. G. Wood's *Out of Doors* (London, 1874)?

"There is a great garret in my little house which is stuffed with books. It was into this that I plunged and rummaged for an hour. At the end of that time I emerged with a little chocolate and silver volume."[1]

Finally, if our assessment of Holmes's attitude towards books is not the correct one, I cannot believe that Watson, his biographer and devoted friend, would have risked giving grave offence by recording in print for posterity his own contemptu-ously off-hand definition of a book collector:

"It struck me that the fellow must be some poor bibliophile who, either as a trade or as a hobby, was a collector of obscure volumes."[2]

[1] *The Lion's Mane*, S., p. 1279.     [2] *The Empty House*, S., p. 563.

# III

## DR. WATSON'S MARRIAGES

IN 1931 the late Sir Sydney Roberts published his *Doctor Watson. Prolegomena to the study of a biographical problem, with a bibliography of Sherlock Holmes.*[1] It was in this booklet of 32 pages, now a rare collector's item, that Watson's learned biographer first drew the attention of Baker Street students to the incontrovertible evidence that the doctor was twice married. It was, of course, already well known that at the conclusion of the Sholto case in July, 1888, Watson had become engaged to Miss Mary Morstan, "a blonde young lady, small, dainty, well gloved and dressed in the most perfect taste",[2] and that the happy couple did not long delay their marriage. In 1893 or early in 1894, however, Mary Watson died. This was firmly established by Holmes's sympathetic remark to Watson in the spring of 1894 on the subject of his old friend's "sad bereavement".[3] Mrs. Watson's father, Captain Morstan of the Indian Army, had "suffered for years from a weak heart", and dropped dead in 1878 as a result of this complaint during "a paroxysm of anger".[4] It seems probable that Mary's sad death at an early age can be explained by a similar weakness inherited from her father and, in the short term, by a matrimonial tiff dith Watson. On the latter point, it may be regarded as suggestive that even before their engagement Miss Morstan showed

---

[1] This essay was reprinted on pp. 60–92 of the same author's *Holmes & Watson. A Miscellany* (1953), henceforward referred to as "Roberts", and for convenience the references that follow are to this later and more accessible work.
[2] *The Sign of Four*, L., p. 152.
[3] *The Empty House*, S., p. 569. "Work is the best antidote to sorrow, my dear Watson."
[4] *The Sign of Four*, L., p. 169.

a tendency to receive well-meant remarks by Watson with "a toss of her proud head".[1]

The evidence of a further Watson marriage in 1902 (or very early in 1903) to which Sir Sydney Roberts drew our attention in 1931[2] is contained in the text of *The Blanched Soldier*, one of the only two accounts of his cases that Holmes wrote himself. He said:

> "I find from my notebook that it was in January, 1903, just after the conclusion of the Boer War, that I had my visit from Mr. James M. Dodd, a big, fresh, sunburned, upstanding Briton. The good Watson had at that time deserted me for a wife, the only selfish action which I can recall in our association. I was alone."[3]

In publishing this discovery Sir Sydney, who was the kindest of men, softened the blow to the pride of his fellow-Sherlockians (all of whom had overlooked what Holmes would have described as "a cock pheasant"[4] of a clue) by conceding modestly that his own attention had been drawn to this significant passage by his friend Mr. Charles Carrington.[5]

The fact of the 1902 marriage has never been disputed, so far as I am aware, since Sir Sydney Roberts revealed it forty years ago, but it cannot be doubted that the discovery came as an unwelcome surprise to many sentimentalists among Watson's admirers. The late Miss Dorothy L. Sayers wrote:

> "When, in 1931, Mr. S. C. Roberts first promulgated the theory of Dr. Watson's second marriage, he created a literary sensation only equalled in recent times by the

[1] *The Sign of Four*, L., p. 217.    [2] Roberts, pp. 87–8.
[3] *The Blanched Soldier*, S., p. 1118. Two years before the appearance of *Dr. Watson*, A. A. Milne published a denial, ostensibly by Watson himself, of any marriage in 1902 or 1903. "My poor wife died in the early 'nineties. For reasons into which I need not go now I did not marry again. Already, as a result of this false publication, I have had an inquiry from the Income Tax Commissioner as to my second wife's independent means, and a circular addressed to Mrs. Watson calling attention to an alleged infallible method, obtained from an unregistered and unqualified Indian sepoy, for removing superfluous hairs." (*By Way of Introduction*, London, 1929, p. 97.) There is no canonical authority for this passage.
[4] *The Three Garridebs*, S., p. 1202. "There have been no advertisements in the agony columns. You know that I miss nothing there. They are my favourite covert for putting up a bird, and I would never have overlooked such a cock pheasant as that."
[5] Roberts, p. 88. In 1931, on p. 27 of his original pamphlet *Dr. Watson*, Sir Sydney had described his friend as "Mr. Charles Edmonds".

exposure of Wordsworth's lapse into frailty and the publication of Charlotte Brontë's love-letters to M. Héger. The first reaction was one of shocked incredulity. Though there is nothing in itself irregular or reprehensible about the remarriage of a widower, we had for so long been accustomed to look upon the good doctor as indissolubly wedded to the memory of Mary Morstan that the suggestion appeared incongruous and distasteful, as though we had detected him in a breach of faith, or, at the very least, of decorum."[1]

Dr. W. S. Bristowe said that "the discovery of a second marriage in 1902, by Mr. Roberts, created a literary sensation only equalled in recent times by the revelations of Boswell's love-life contained in his long-lost diaries".[2]

With respect, I think it fair to say that to the objective and experienced observer, tolerant of human frailty, the revelation that Watson's preoccupation with the attractions of the opposite sex was still sufficiently intense to tempt him into further matrimonial adventure at the age of fifty (he was born in 1852), should have come as no surprise. Before his marriage to Mary Morstan he admitted that he had enjoyed "an experience of women which extends over many nations and three separate continents".[3] He had clearly benefited from this experience. It would be idle to speculate about the probable speed of Watson's wooing of Mary Morstan had this been in progress today, but it is noteworthy that even in the non-permissive society of 1888 he admitted to his indulgence in "dangerous thoughts" about her in a matter of minutes after their first meeting,[4] and that he was holding her hand by the evening of the same day.[5] It was not without good reason that Holmes, a psychologist of unequalled penetration, summed up his best friend's propensities in a single appropriately mild but significant phrase. "Now, Watson, the fair sex is your department".[6]

Watson's virile interest in attractive women is self-evident throughout the entire canon. As early as 1889 he thought that Miss Turner of Boscombe Valley was "one of the most lovely

---

[1] *Unpopular Opinions* (London, 1946), p. 152.
[2] *The Sherlock Holmes Journal*, December, 1954, p. 28.
[3] *The Sign of Four*, L., p. 152.    [4] *Ibid.*, p. 158.    [5] *Ibid.*, p. 177.
[6] *The Second Stain*, S., p. 871.

young women I have ever seen in my life".[1] If it be urged by the
sentimentalists that this expression was merely one of innocent
admiration, my answer would be that I would be justifiably
shocked if it were anything else. The old Adam in Watson was
temporarily sleeping for an entirely natural reason. At this
precise time he was in the transports of the first months of his
marriage to Mary Morstan. It will be recalled that Watson
recorded that "we were seated at breakfast, my wife and I,
when the maid brought in a telegram".[2] It was from Holmes,
inviting his biographer to accompany him to the West of England to save Miss Turner's sweetheart, James McCarthy, from
the gallows.

After Mary's death, however, there can be little doubt about
the full-blooded nature of Watson's "dangerous thoughts"
about women, and this was especially true of the emotions that
he recorded in his accounts of Holmes's cases grouped around
the turn of the century. Of Lady Mary Brackenstall he said,
"Seldom have I seen so graceful a figure, so womanly a presence
and so beautiful a face".[3] It may be thought to be of psychological interest that Watson placed Lady Mary's graceful
figure first and her beautiful face last in listing the ingredients
of the appeal she had for him. During the investigation of the
death of Mrs. J. Neil Gibson, Watson enthusiastically described
the attractions of the governess, a "beautiful woman" with a
"noble figure", and said that he would "never forget the effect
which Miss Dunbar produced upon me".[4] In the Maberley
affair, he positively dilated upon the "perfect figure" and the
"wonderful Spanish eyes" (in that order of preference) of
Isadora Klein.[5] It seems perfectly obvious, now that we have
assembled the evidence, that Watson was ripe for another
incursion into marriage by 1902. It is not too much to say,
indeed, that we might reasonably have expected an abandon-
ment of his life of continence as a widower at Baker Street at
a much earlier date.

Who was the Mrs. Watson of 1902 or early 1903? Sir
Sydney Roberts attached importance to the fact that the case

[1] *The Boscombe Valley Mystery*, S., p. 85.      [2] *Ibid.*, p. 75.
[3] *The Abbey Grange*, S., p. 835.      [4] *Thor Bridge*, S., p. 1235.
[5] *The Three Gables*, S., p. 1174.

involving the rescue of "Violet de Merville, young, rich, beautiful, accomplished, a wonder-woman in every way" from "the clutches of a fiend", Baron Adelbert Gruner, took place at the beginning of September 1902.[1] Sir Sydney wrote:

> "After the terrible exposure of the true character of her *fiancé*, what more natural than that Watson should, after a fitting interval, make inquiries as to her recovery of health and spirits? Furthermore, had not Watson acquired a peculiar technique, so to speak, in his previous courtship of Miss Morstan? It may be objected that Miss de Merville moved in exalted circles, and that a retired practitioner would not have the *droit d'entrée* to her society. But here a significant fact must be considered. Miss de Merville's father was a soldier, and a soldier who had won distinction in Afghanistan —'de Merville of Khyber fame'.[2] With such a father-in-law Watson would at once be on common ground."[3]

A year after Sir Sydney had published this interesting theory, it was subjected to severe criticism by Mr. Thomas S. Blakeney. In his biography of Holmes he devoted part of the first Appendix to the exposition of eight points which seemed to him entirely to demolish the possibility of Sir Sydney's conjecture having any foundation in fact. The citing of the first is perhaps sufficient to exemplify the seriousness of Mr. Blakeney's objections:

> " 'What more natural', asks Mr. Roberts, than that Watson should call upon Miss de Merville after the episode of Baron Gruner was over, to inquire after her health and spirits? What more unusual, we suggest, seeing that he had never met her. It was Holmes who interviewed her, not Watson."[4]

Mr. Blakeney's eighth point must be quoted, for it was the only one to which Sir Sydney replied:

> "Finally, would a chivalrous man like Watson be likely to prepare for publication a full account of an incident which would ever be a shame-faced memory to Violet de Merville, if he were her husband? Surely, she could only wish that the subject was never mentioned again to her; can we believe a

---

[1] *The Illustrious Client*, S., pp. 1089 and 1092.
[2] *Ibid.*, p. 1092.      [3] Roberts, p. 89.      [4] Blakeney, p. 113.

loyal husband would disregard her wish, either in her lifetime or after?"[1]

In 1934, two years after the publication of Mr. Blakeney's book, Sir Sydney wrote:

"Elsewhere (*Dr. Watson*, pp. 27 ff.) I have suggested that Miss de Merville afterwards became the second wife of Dr. Watson. Critics have dismissed this theory as fantastic or even as negligible, sometimes with a greater measure of scorn than of argument. The objection that Watson would not have cared to record his wife's early misfortunes is certainly valid, but it should be remembered (*a*) that the story was not published for twenty years after the events described; (*b*) that Watson may have disguised the surname in his narrative. If my theory is correct, it may well be that the unusually fervid description owes something to Watson's own feelings."[2]

The late Gavin Brend agreed with Mr. Blakeney, adding that "It is equally unlikely that [Watson] married any of the other unattached ladies referred to in his narratives. A strong case can be made against any one of them."[3] Dr. W. S. Bristowe observed briefly that "attempts made by biographers to identify [the Mrs. Watson of 1902] as one of the women mentioned in any of the adventures in which [Watson] was associated with Holmes are fruitless".[4] On the other hand, Mr. George Haynes has more recently told us, with the brevity of conviction, that "in 1902 Dr. Watson married Lady Frances Carfax, sole survivor of the Earl of Rufton".[5]

Mr. Haynes's assertion, if I understand him aright, is based in part upon the fact that Watson never saw Lady Frances in the flesh until the long search for her on the Continent was over and she had been saved "from the evil designs of the Schlesingers [*sic*] of Adelaide". He considers that Watson's emotions during the period when she was but a name to him can be compared, as he puts it, with those of the "classical professor who fell in love with a statue of a Greek goddess on whom he was doing a paper". Mr. Haynes goes on:

---

[1] Blakeney, p. 114.  [2] *Baker Street Studies*, p. 192.  [3] Brend, p. 170.
[4] *SHJ*, December, 1954, p. 29.  [5] *Ibid.*, Spring, 1963, p. 53.

"Dr. Watson came face to face with the lady at last under the most extraordinary circumstances and had to exert his every effort as a physician to keep her from dying in his arms. This was certainly the final force of his attraction to her and the beginning of her consciousness of him. He describes her with these few words: '. . . a statuesque face (Shades of the professor of the classics!) of a woman in middle age'.[1] That is all."[2]

In my view Mr. Haynes does himself less than justice in his assembly of the evidence in support of these pleasing conjectures. Before Watson set out for Lausanne, the first stage in his quest for Lady Frances, it was impressed upon him by Holmes that she was "a beautiful woman, still in fresh middle age".[3] Upon arrival at the National Hotel at Lausanne, Watson was told by "M. Moser, the well-known manager" that Lady Frances "was not more than forty. She was still handsome, and bore every sign of having in her youth been a very lovely woman."[4] Mr. Haynes might also have quite properly drawn to our attention a further point which would not have diminished the interest of Watson, the owner of "a depleted bank account",[5] in Lady Frances Carfax:

"M. Moser knew nothing of any valuable jewellery but it had been remarked by the servants that the heavy trunk in the lady's bedroom was always scrupulously locked."[6]

Despite all this, I do not think that Mr. Haynes has made out his case, for he appears to have overlooked a fact that may be thought to demolish everything he says. The Hon. Philip Green, "a huge, swarthy man with a bristling black beard", confessed to Holmes and Watson that "there never was in this world a man who loved a woman"[7] as he loved Lady Frances, who in her turn loved him sufficiently "to remain single all her sainted days"[8] following his departure to South Africa. The case had reunited the devoted couple. It follows that Mr.

---

[1] Presumably an inexact reference to *Lady Frances Carfax*, S., p. 1038. Watson's actual description was "the statuesque face of a handsome and spiritual woman of middle age".
[2] *SHJ*, December, 1954, p. 53.　　　[3] *Lady Frances Carfax*, S., p. 1020.
[4] *Ibid.*, p. 1021.　　　[5] *The Cardboard Box*, S., p. 924.
[6] *Lady Frances Carfax*, S., p. 1021.　　　[7] *Ibid.*, p. 1026.　　[8] *Ibid.*, p. 1027.

Haynes's idyllic description of the subsequent married life of Watson and Lady Frances, whilst demonstrating the author's enviable imagination and literary skill, is unhappily beside the point:

> "So, we have a vision of two greying people, clinging to each other, a little wrinkled but young at heart, sipping wine beneath the stars of Paris, riding through the frosty night in a sled in Switzerland, reading and writing poetry in a sunny Italian villa, and planting flowers in their lovely garden in Sussex."[1]

I do not think that Sir Sydney Roberts had any reason to be disturbed by these criticisms. The identification of Miss Violet de Merville as Watson's bride of 1902 was perhaps unduly reckless and was justifiably exploded, but his revelation of the marriage itself was solid and could not be disputed. He had, moreover, directly stimulated the investigation of Watson's sex life by other scholars. In 1932 the late Harold W. Bell, whilst accepting as an established fact Watson's nuptials in 1902, insisted upon treating this ceremony as "Dr. Watson's Third Marriage"[2] in his exhaustive *Sherlock Holmes and Dr. Watson. The Chronology of their Adventures*. He advanced the theory that Watson's real second marriage took place in 1896,[3] only two or three years after the death of Mary Watson.

The evidence upon which Bell relied in support of his suggestion was limited to several extracts from the texts of *The Veiled Lodger* and *Lady Frances Carfax*. The relevant sentences from the first of these two sources are:

> "One forenoon—it was late in 1896—I received a hurried note from Holmes asking for my attendance" and "Two days later, when I called upon my friend . . ."[4]

It was perfectly logical for Bell to have concluded from this

---

[1] *SHJ*, December, 1954, p. 54. Mr. Haynes implies in a footnote on the same page that all this travel and gracious living was accomplished on the proceeds of the sale of Lady Frances Carfax's jewels, which "were, of course, very valuable".

[2] *Chronology*, p. 113. Bell summarily dismissed Sir Sydney Roberts's theory involving Miss de Merville as "playful conjecture", and suggested (on the basis of some exceedingly tenuous evidence in *The Mazarin Stone* which need not detain us) that there was "a slight indication" that the unknown lady might have been connected with the stage.

[3] "On Dr. Watson's Second Marriage", *Chronology*, pp. 91–5.

[4] *The Veiled Lodger*, S., pp. 1288 and 1300.

that in 1896 Watson had deserted Holmes and the beloved and familiar rooms in Baker Street and was living elsewhere. What was the reason? I agree with Bell that Watson could not have been on holiday, either abroad or in "the glades of the New Forest" or on "the shingle of Southsea".[1] This is demonstrated by the fact that when the "hurried note" from Holmes arrived, Watson was sufficiently close at hand to join his friend before the client, Mrs. Merrilow of South Brixton, "an elderly, motherly woman of the buxom landlady type",[2] had finished her story, and soon enough to take luncheon (accompanied by a bottle of Montrachet) with Holmes.[3] We can be quite certain, too, that Watson did not leave Baker Street in 1896 to resume the practice of medicine, as Bell pointed out, for in the following year he referred lugubriously to "the degree in which I had lost touch with my profession".[4]

Holmes's most famous maxim, and certainly his favourite (Watson recorded his use of it on at least five occasions) was, "When you have eliminated the impossible, whatever remains, *however improbable*, must be the truth".[5] It may be thought, therefore, that Bell's argument, "The only conceivable [remaining] motive for [Watson's] desertion of Holmes, and the life and activities which had hitherto absorbed him, is marriage"[6] was solidly based (although he did not say so) on the best traditions of the canon. I find myself very much in accord with this hypothesis, for I have already said that the evidence assembled in regard to Watson's marked sexual proclivities strongly suggests that he would have succumbed to the temptation before 1902. He was at the dangerous age of forty-four in 1896, and doubtless felt that both youth and opportunity were slipping away from him. In the previous year Watson had confessed to Holmes that he had taken a Turkish

---

[1] *The Cardboard Box*, S., p. 924. It will be recalled that these were the places for which Watson, a Hampshire man, always yearned during the holiday season.
[2] *The Veiled Lodger*, S., p. 1288.          [3] *Ibid.*, p. 1294.
[4] *The Missing Three-Quarter*, S., p. 821.
[5] *The Sign of Four*, L., p. 185. In the same case (p. 148) Holmes reduced it to "Eliminate all other factors, and the one which remains must be the truth". In repeating it more or less exactly in *The Beryl Coronet*, S., p. 273 and *The Bruce-Partington Plans*, S., pp. 990–1, he referred to it as "an old maxim of mine" and "the old axiom". In *The Blanched Soldier*, S., p. 1138 he used it almost word for word as he had done in *The Sign of Four*.
[6] *Chronology*, p. 91.

bath "because for the last few days I have been feeling rheumatic and old".[1]

Bell found further support for his hypothesis in the text of *Lady Frances Carfax*, a case which preceded that of *The Veiled Lodger*:

> "In it we are given an unmistakable hint of what is toward, as if Watson, discreetly breaking through his usual reticence, were preparing his readers for a change in his circumstances. Holmes, 'with a mischievous twinkle', asks him: 'Who shared your cab in your drive this morning?' and Watson parries the question, as he himself notes, 'with some asperity'. Holmes then proceeds to deduce from the splashes on Watson's coat that he had occupied the left side of the hansom—which, of course, is where he would have sat if his companion had been a lady.[2] If Holmes had not suspected as much, his insistence would have been the idlest curiosity, and his mischievous twinkle merely stupid; while Watson's asperity would have been wholly uncalled for."[3]

Bell made two further points in his dissertation, which I shall take the liberty of amplifying in one or two particulars. If it be urged that Watson nowhere directly mentioned his marriage of 1896, it is relevant to recall his similar odd reticence in regard to the undisputed marriage of 1902, about which, as Bell pointed out, we should have known nothing had it not been for Holmes's reference to it in *The Blanched Soldier*.[4] The second point was a proper inference from Watson's own words:

> "Mr. Sherlock Holmes was in active practice for twenty-three years,[5] and . . . during seventeen of these I was allowed to co-operate with him and keep notes."[6]

Bell's argument relied in part upon the assumption that the co-operation ended in the late summer of 1902. At "the latter end of June, 1902, shortly after the conclusion of the South African War", Watson was unquestionably still at Baker

---

[1] *Lady Frances Carfax*, S., p. 1018.
[2] *Ibid.*, pp. 1018–19.
[3] *Chronology*, pp. 92–3.                 *Ibid.*, p. 95.
[5] From 1877 to 1891 and from 1894 to 1903.
[6] *The Veiled Lodger*, S., p. 1287.

Street.[1] By "September 3, 1902, the day when my narrative begins", however, Watson had finally parted from Holmes, and was living in his own establishment "in Queen Anne Street".[2] It may be presumed that at this time the 1902 marriage had taken place, or was imminent.

The sad finality of Watson's departure from Baker Street during July or August, 1902, is further demonstrated by the fact that in the following year, "one Sunday evening early in September of the year 1903", Watson received a laconic message, "Come at once if convenient—if inconvenient come all the same.—S.H."[3] On his arrival at Baker Street, Holmes "greeted me back to what had once been my home". Watson had resumed medical practice, and was initially annoyed to discover that Holmes's purpose was to seek his view on the habits of "Professor Presbury's faithful wolf-hound, Roy". It was "in some disappointment" that Watson asked himself, "Was it for so trivial a question as this that I had been summoned from my work?"[4] Although the reunion ended happily enough, the nostalgic reflection that the old days had gone forever must have been sharpened for Watson by Holmes's remark that he now relied for his every-day assistance upon a person called Mercer, whom Watson had not met. " 'Mercer is since your time', said Holmes. 'He is my general utility man who looks up routine business'. "[5] The shadows were lengthening in Baker Street itself, moreover, for Watson recorded that the affair of Professor Presbury and his dog was "one of the very last cases handled by Holmes before his retirement".[6]

With 1902 as the year in which the regular co-operation ended now established, it will be seen that since Holmes and Watson first joined forces in 1881, the year of the Jefferson Hope case, if allowance is made for the hiatus of three years (May 1891 to April 1894) when Holmes was out of England and presumed dead, the period of co-operation was eighteen years on the face of it. Since Watson said flatly that it was

[1] *The Three Garridebs*, S., p. 1197. "Holmes had spent several days in bed, as was his habit from time to time, but he emerged that morning with a long foolscap document in his hand."
[2] *The Illustrious Client*, S., pp. 1089–90.   [3] *The Creeping Man*, S., p. 1244.
[4] *Ibid.*, p. 1245.   [5] *Ibid.*, p. 1258.
[6] *Ibid.*, p. 1244. Holmes's "active practice for twenty-three years" was, of course, from 1877 to 1903, less the gap of three years from 1891 to 1894.

seventeen years, the arithmetic is apparently out by one year, as Bell observed.[1] The interruption of the partnership for the greater part of 1896 neatly disposes of this difficulty.

It is noteworthy, in further support of Bell's argument, that apart from *The Veiled Lodger*, which occurred "late in 1896", there is no record of any other case in that year in which Watson was involved, so that it is reasonable to presume that Watson devoted himself to his new marital duties with single-minded vigour and diligence. It would be idle to speculate whether this had any connexion with the new Mrs. Watson's death after only a year of marriage. However that may be, by the earliest days of 1897 ("on a bitterly cold and frosty morning", in fact) Watson, once more a widower, was back in his old bedroom at Baker Street:

"I was wakened by a tugging at my shoulder. It was Holmes. The candle in his hand shone upon his eager, stooping face, and told me at a glance that something was amiss."[2]

It seems to me to be of the highest significance, and surely indicative of Holmes's relief at having his old friend back once more under the roof of Baker Street, that on this single occasion in the entire canon the great detective expressed himself in impromptu but graceful verse, despite his more usual antipathy towards poetry.[3]

" 'Come, Watson, come!' he cried. 'The game is afoot. Not a word! Into your clothes and come!' "[4]

In view of Holmes's previous concern that his biographer should try to forget his grief at the loss of Mary Watson, by actively joining him in the Adair case in 1894 ("Work is the best antidote to sorrow, my dear Watson"),[5] it may be thought that Holmes's summons to him "late in 1896" to come round to Baker Street, followed the same kindly pattern. If this is right, and the real reason for the "hurried note" was that Holmes had recently learnt of Mrs. Watson's death, the incident demonstrates his thoughtful affection for his friend,[6] for Holmes

[1] *Chronology*, pp. 94–5.    [2] *The Abbey Grange*, S., p. 833.
[3] *The Retired Colourman*, S., p. 1321. " 'Cut out the poetry, Watson',; Holmes severely".
[4] *The Abbey Grange*, S., p. 833.    [5] *The Empty House*, S., p. 569.
[6] *The Veiled Lodger*, S., p. 1288.

was in no need of Watson's help. As the latter recorded, the case of Mrs. Eugenia Ronder, although one of "the most terrible human tragedies", was not even a matter that offered "Holmes the opportunity of showing [his] curious gifts of instinct and observation".[1] All the two friends had to do was to listen with sympathy to Mrs. Ronder's story, and tactfully persuade her not to commit suicide. The old campaigner's active assistance, with "my revolver in my pocket and the thrill of adventure in my heart",[2] was not necessary on this occasion.

I have devoted some little space to Bell's theory of "Dr. Watson's Second Marriage" (as he called it) in 1896, because I believe that it is well founded. I have added some documentary evidence of my own in its support, simply because Bell was subjected to fierce criticism in regard to his discovery, most of which was emotional rather than objective. The late Gavin Brend's outburst, "After all, we are dealing with John H. Watson, M.D.—not with Bluebeard",[3] whilst doubtless sincere, was scarcely evidential. It was, of course, entirely to be expected that the sentimentalists, faced with this new revelation only a year after their reluctant but unavoidable acceptance of the 1902 marriage, would be horrified at the suggestion of yet another. Their arguments, however, were not convincing. Brend said, for example, that "a succession of such short-lived marriages seems on the face of it improbable."[4] This was a reckless *non sequitur*, for it is surely obvious that the more short-lived a man's marriages may be, the greater the number of such unions he can include in a lifetime, assuming that he has the stamina and enthusiasm which Dr. Watson clearly enjoyed. With Brend's credibility thus shaken, we are entitled to reject his conclusion, "Reluctantly we fear that this romantic theory of a third Mrs. Watson must be jettisoned."[5]

Miss Dorothy Sayers was clearly very cross indeed with Bell:

> "Within a year, the critics had accepted the second marriage, and one of them—a prey to that fury of iconoclasm

[1] *The Veiled Lodger*, p. 1288.    [2] *The Empty House*, S., p. 570.
[3] Brend, pp. 141–2.    [4] *Ibid.*, p. 141.
[5] Brend, p. 142. Brend frankly conceded (p. 141) that the only reference made by Watson to the year 1896 was in *The Veiled Lodger*.

which urges us to dance upon the fragments of a fallen idol and grind them, if possible, to powder—had come forward with the hypothesis of yet a third Watson marriage.

*Quousque tandem* . . . ? Are a fourth and a fifth Mrs. Watson to be disinterred from nameless graves in obscure paragraphs in order that each fresh commentator may show himself a more avid ghoul than his predecessors? Is every blank page in Watson's notebook to be filled with a conjectural marriage certificate? Or is it possible to check this itch of match-making and forbid, in the words of a poet who owes his sole fame to the brutality of his critic, the 'red and raging eye' of imagination to pry further?"[1]

I intend to take up Miss Sayers's challenge. Before discussing the remarkable discovery which concludes this essay, however, I hope that I may at least minimally reduce the storm of criticism I shall attract by adding to the existing published evidence of my constant willingness to defend Watson against insinuations regarding his supposed extra-marital affairs with women. In this context I found myself in agreement with Miss Sayers and at variance with both Bell and Sir Sydney Roberts. I wrote:

"On the subject of the undoubted attractions of Miss Hunter, H. W. Bell suggested (*Chronology*, p. 68) that Watson, 'always a ladies' man' despite his marriage to the devoted Miss Mary Morstan, started up a later correspondence with Miss Hunter with an eye to the main chance. The evidence advanced for this lewd suggestion was Watson's knowledge that she later became the headmistress of a private school in Walsall. This quite shocking insinuation was sternly rebutted by Miss Dorothy Sayers (*Unpopular Opinions*, p. 160) who pointed out that it was much more probable that it was Miss Hunter who had an eye to the main chance and sent Watson, a possible future father, a prospectus of her school."[2]

And again:

---

[1] *Unpopular Opinions*, op. cit., p. 152. Miss Sayers, like Bell's other critics, conceded the accuracy of the revelation made by Sir Sydney Roberts. She wrote, "The evidence for *one* marriage after the death of Mary Watson (*née* Morstan) in 1891–4 is, so far as it goes, substantial . . . I shall make no attempt to upset the 1902 marriage." (pp. 152 & 153.)

[2] Hall, pp. 135–6.

"Sir Sydney implied (Roberts, pp. 71–2) that whilst in India Watson may have found opportunities for sexual adventure among the staff-nurses at the Base Hospital at Peshawur. Against this attractive theory must be set the fact that Watson, according to his own account in *A Study in Scarlet*, was 'worn with pain' and later 'so weak and emaciated' following an attack of enteric fever 'that a medical board determined that not a day should be lost in sending him home to England.' "[1]

Perhaps I may add to the lustre of my small halo in this regard by recording that I also disagree entirely with the innuendoes made in 1934 by Miss Helen Simpson in regard to the apparent anomaly in Watson's professional career in 1878, the year in which he himself said "I took my degree of Doctor of Medicine of the University of London".[2] In a thoughtful essay "Medical Career and Capacities of Dr. J. H. Watson",[3] Miss Simpson said that it was distinctly odd that Watson, having gained the degree of M.D. (London), an extremely difficult one to obtain, and having held for an unknown period the enviable post of house-physician or surgeon at St. Bartholomew's Hospital,[4] should then train at Netley for service in the Army Medical Department, where, in peacetime, his principal duties would have been the inspection of latrines and feet. Miss Simpson wrote:

"At once a contradiction becomes apparent, when we consider that such achievements [Watson's M.D. and his post at Bart's] indicate a considerable degree of distinction in the profession of medicine, and that the Army Medical Department was at that time regarded as a dead end. The black silk gown, and hood of scarlet cloth lined with violet silk, is only conferred, after the M.B. has been taken, upon the presenter of a thesis of outstanding merit. The hospital posts were, and still are, sought only by ambitious men, awarded only to men of marked competence. Watson evidently had his foot upon the first rung of the ladder. What impelled him to descend, to abandon ambition for obscurity?"[5]

[1] Hall, p. 137.   [2] *A Study in Scarlet*, L., p. 5.
[3] *Baker Street Studies*, pp. 37–61.
[4] *A Study in Scarlet*, L., p. 6. "I recognised young Stamford, who had been a dresser under me at Bart's."
[5] *Baker Street Studies*, pp. 37–8.

PLATE III. The neolithic dwelling on Dartmoor
(*see p.* 21)

PLATE IV. Holmes's homemade encyclopaedia
(*see p.* 28)

To Miss Simpson, these circumstances seemed imbued with sinister significance, and sex reared its head. She raised the question of Watson's possible activities among the young nurses at Bart's, as Sir Sydney Roberts had done in regard to the nurses at the Base Hospital in India. Without making any direct accusation, she suggested a possible solution to the problem she herself had posed:

> "The morals of their juniors are no concern of the seniors in a hospital; but we may, by no great stretch of the imagination, visualise some frailer member of the other sex making charges against Watson, either with a view to blackmail or revenge . . . Watson himself is silent, merely giving the undeniable facts of his early success with an account of subsequent deliberate steps taken to quit the country."[1]

I agree that there is something to be explained, but I feel that this picture of Watson as a seducer, leaving England and his professional career to avoid the consequences of his supposedly unseemly behaviour at Bart's, was going altogether too far. It ignored completely the very human reason for Watson joining the Army Medical Department advanced by Sir Sydney Roberts three years earlier, which disposed of Miss Simpson's innuendoes. Sir Sydney wrote:

> "It may at first sight seem strange that Watson should have chosen the career of an army surgeon, but after what has already been said about Watson's colonial background,[2] it is clear that in the full vigour of early manhood he could not face the humdrum life of the general practitioner. The appeal of a full, pulsing life of action, coupled with the camaraderie of a regimental mess, was irresistible. Accordingly, we find him proceeding to the army surgeon's course at Netley."[3]

I deplore, too, the sinister interpretation Mr. John Dickson Carr, the biographer of Watson's literary agent, placed upon

---

[1] *Baker Street Studies*, p. 39.

[2] Watson's boyhood was partly spent in Australia. He said to Miss Morstan as they stood hand in hand among "the great rubbish-heaps" in the grounds of Pondicherry Lodge, "It looks as though all the moles in England had been let loose in it. I have seen something of the sort on the side of a hill near Ballarat, where the prospectors had been at work." (*The Sign of Four*, L., p. 178.)

[3] Roberts, p. 66.

his discovery of the unpublished manuscript of *Angels of Darkness*, in "three exercise books bound in thick cardboard", which Watson had understandably never allowed to be printed. It dealt with a previously unknown period of Watson's life from the spring of 1884 to the summer of 1886, which he spent in the United States. Carr wrote:

"Watson, in fact, once practised medicine in San Francisco. And his reticence can be understood; he acted discreditably. Those who have suspected Watson of black perfidy in his relations with women will find their worst suspicions justified. Either he had a wife before he married Mary Morstan, or else he heartlessly jilted the poor girl whom he holds in his arms as the curtain falls on *Angels of Darkness*. The name of the girl? There lies our difficulty. To give her name, a well-known one, would be to betray the author as well as the character. At best it would impeach Watson in matters other than matrimonial."[1]

The late W. S. Baring-Gould subsequently did some admirable research on this episode.[2] The evidence contained in the three exercise books and the fact of Watson's stay in America (he recorded no cases in which he and Holmes were involved during the relevant period) could not be denied. Baring-Gould's inquiries, however, showed that Watson had behaved throughout like an ex-officer and a gentleman, as we would expect. Watson's elder and "unhappy brother" was involved. This gentleman, it will be recalled, was left with good prospects, but "threw away his chances, lived for some time in poverty with occasional short intervals of prosperity, and, finally, taking to drink" died prior to the Sholto case in 1888.[3]

In 1884 Watson, whose family relationships were admirable but whose bank account was frequently depleted,[4] borrowed a

---

[1] *The Life of Sir Arthur Conan Doyle* (London, 1949), pp. 92–3.

[2] Baring-Gould, pp. 58–9.

[3] *The Sign of Four*, L., p. 150. It will be recalled that Watson inherited his brother's watch, which Holmes demonstrated had been repeatedly pawned and redeemed during its previous ownership.

[4] *The Cardboard Box*, S., p. 924. This was doubtless due to Watson spending half his pension on racing (*Shoscombe Old Place*, S., p. 1301) which caused Holmes so much concern at one period that he kept Watson's cheque-book under lock and key. (*The Dancing Men*, S., p. 611.)

substantial sum of money from Holmes and sailed on an errand of mercy to San Francisco, where his brother was penniless and seriously ill. Whilst nursing his brother slowly back to temporary health, Watson established himself in medical practice in order to earn enough money to repay his debt to Holmes. One of the first of his patients was Miss Constance Adams of San Francisco, aged twenty-seven, an incurably ailing girl who had been unsuccessfully treated by all the established local physicians. Despite her illness, she was possessed of delicate physical attractions which had a strong appeal for Watson. They fell deeply in love and were married despite Constance's short expectation of life.[1] All Baker Street students owe Baring-Gould a debt of gratitude for his work in thus disposing of the unworthy suggestion that Watson had "acted discreditably" and may have "heartlessly jilted the poor girl".[2]

Probably because of his wish not to harrow our feelings more than necessary, and possibly because as a meticulous biographer he did not wish to mix speculation with the solid facts he had unearthed, Baring-Gould did not mention the death of Constance Watson. It was, of course, calmly and courageously expected, and in any event Watson's engagement to Mary Morstan in July, 1888, provides the sad proof of its actuality. As to the date of Constance's death, we are fortunate indeed, to have from Baring-Gould himself the date of October, 1886, for both *The Noble Bachelor* and *The Second Stain*.[3] In these two affairs Watson was respectively "sharing rooms with Holmes in Baker Street"[4] and receiving, with Holmes, "two visitors of European fame within the walls of our humble room in Baker Street".[5] It is clear, therefore, that Watson, by now a widower for the first time, had sadly returned from America to repay his debt to Holmes and was back in his old quarters. Constance had died in America (clearly her health would not have allowed a voyage to England) either earlier in 1886 or in the latter part of 1885, assuming that Watson would require some months

---

[1] Baring-Gould, pp. 58–9.    [2] Carr, *op. cit.*, pp. 92–3.
[3] Baring-Gould, p. 60.
[4] *The Noble Bachelor*, S., p. 224. It is of crucial importance to the inquiry that follows that Watson said that this case took place 'a few weeks before my own marriage".
[5] *The Second Stain*, S., p. 859.

to sell his practice and clear up his other affairs in San Francisco.

We have now established for the first time that Watson was married on at least four occasions, i.e. in 1884–5, in 1888–9, in 1896 and in 1902, and that Miss Constance Adams of San Francisco was his earliest bride. Dorothy Sayers's challenge, however, which I said I would take up, was in precise numerical terms:

"*Quousque tandem . . .?* Are a fourth and a fifth Mrs. Watsons to be disinterred from nameless graves in obscure paragraphs in order that each fresh commentator may show himself a more avid ghoul than his predecessors?"[1]

It is a great nuisance that before proceeding with the main theme of this essay, I must dispose once and for all of the arguments of those commentators who have not accepted that the case of *The Sign of Four* and Watson's engagement to Mary Morstan took place in July, 1888. In underlining this definite dating, which in my already expressed view is not arguable,[2] I have the firm support of the two principal Baker Street biographers, Mr. T. S. Blakeney and the late W. S. Baring-Gould. Blakeney said that "*The Sign of Four* is more amply authenticated than any other case of Sherlock Holmes. Only the strongest proof of its inaccuracy can over-throw the dating of 1888, and such proof we contend, is lacking".[3] Baring-Gould gave a firm date of September, 1888, in his biography of Sherlock Holmes in 1962,[4] and six years later remarked that most students "are now agreed that the proper year of *The Sign of Four* is 1888".[5] The same learned author, incidentally, placed the Watson/Morstan marriage in May, 1889. It would be unnecessary to say more, had not Sir Sydney Roberts and the late H. W. Bell recorded their differing opinions that the correct year of *The Sign of Four* was 1886[6] and 1887.[7]

I am in sympathy with those students of the canon who find the calculating of the dates of the cases to be an irritation, and

[1] *Unpopular Opinions*, p. 152.      [2] Hall, p. 109.
[3] Blakeney, p. 58.      [4] Baring-Gould, p. 108.
[5] *The Annotated Sherlock Holmes* (2 vols., London, 1968) i, p. 325.
[6] Roberts, p. 75.      [7] *Chronology*, p. 38.

who regard as virtually unreadable by the layman such almost purely mathematical dissertations as Dorothy Sayers's "The Dates in *The Red-Headed League*".[1] It is therefore fortunate that no arithmetical agility is required to establish the fact that 1888 was the date of the Sholto case.

When Miss Morstan came to see Holmes and Watson on 8 July, 1888,[2] she told them that an advertisement addressed to her by name had appeared in *The Times* "about six years ago— to be exact upon the 4th of May, 1882."[3] During the same conversation she said that her father, Captain Morstan, had "disappeared upon the 3rd of December, 1878—nearly ten years ago."[4] Miss Morstan told the two friends that she was seventeen when her father vanished in 1878, and after she had left Baker Street one of Watson's "dangerous thoughts" about her was that "she must be seven-and-twenty now—a sweet age, when youth has lost its self-consciousness and become a little sobered by experience".[5]

All this is so clear and precise that one might initially wonder why Roberts and Bell allowed themselves to become confused. It must be said in justice to two great Baker Street scholars that Watson himself muddled his account rather badly a few pages farther on by describing the events of the night of 8 July as having occurred on "a September evening, and not yet seven o'clock".[6] This was, of course, a patent mistake, but it has been seized upon by enthusiastic biographers as a basis upon which superstructures of learned speculation have been built, as we have seen. The truth of the matter, I feel sure, is to be found in another remark by Watson on the same evening which resolves the whole problem:

"Miss Morstan's demeanour was as resolute and collected as ever. I endeavoured to cheer and amuse her by reminiscences of my adventures in Afghanistan; but, to tell the truth, I was myself so excited at our situation, and so curious as to our destination, that my stories were slightly involved. To this day she declares that I told her one moving anecdote

---

[1] *Unpopular Opinions*, pp. 168–76.
[2] *The Sign of Four*, L., p. 155. Miss Morstan brought with her a letter postmarked 7 July which she had received that morning.
[3] *Ibid.*, p. 154.     [4] *Ibid.*, p. 154.     [5] *Ibid.*, pp. 157-8.
[6] *Ibid.*, p. 160.

as to how a musket looked into my tent at the dead of night, and how I fired a double-barrelled tiger cub at it."[1]

There was, of course, another reason why Watson was talking nonsense, on his own confession. He was extremely susceptible to the charms of the opposite sex, as we have seen, and he left us in no doubt about the immediate effect upon him of Miss Morstan's subtle attractions, "her smiles, the deep rich tones of her voice, [and] the strange mystery which overhung her life".[2] He was completely bowled over, of course. In Yorkshire villages, such as the one in which I live, we say indulgently of a man in this state of mind that he "does not know whether it is Tuesday or whether it is raining", which is very apposite as regards Watson's mental condition on 8 July, 1888. I can see no difference in the outward symptoms of confusing muskets with tiger cubs and mixing up July and September.

Watson's remark, however, that Miss Morstan "was as resolute and collected as ever" was very significant, as was Holmes's admiring comment about her at the end of the case:

> "She . . . might have been most useful in such work as we have been doing. She had a decided genius that way; witness the way in which she preserved that Agra plan from all the other papers of her father."[3]

It was from the calm and precise Miss Morstan and the letter she produced, and not from the confused and lovesick Watson that we can confidently accept the conclusive evidence that the case of *The Sign of Four* took place in July, 1888.

With all this cleared up and established, we can now examine the facts of Watson's true second marriage, which was sandwiched between October, 1886, when we know Constance Watson was definitely dead and Watson himself (widowed for the first time) was back in Baker Street, and July, 1888, when Watson was ripe for his third matrimonial venture. The first thing we can be sure about is that the second marriage took place

---

[1] *The Sign of Four*, p. 162. Watson recorded that while in this confused state of mind he also offered some odd medical advice to the "confirmed hypochondriac", Mr. Thaddeus Sholto. "Holmes declares that he overheard me caution him against the great danger of taking more than two drops of castor-oil, while I recommended strychnine in large doses as a sedative." (*Ibid.*, p. 174).
[2] *Ibid.*, p. 157.  [3] *Ibid.*, L., p. 270.

during November or December, 1886, for we know that in October, 1886, Watson recorded that this was "a few weeks before my own marriage".[1] We also know with certainty that the second Mrs. Watson was still alive in September, 1887, from conclusive evidence in Watson's record of the tragic case of John Openshaw and the Ku Klux Klan, which took place in that month.[2] Watson wrote:

"The year '87 furnished us with a long series of cases of greater or less interest, of which I retain the records . . . It was in the latter days of September, and the equinoctial gales had set in with exceptional violence. All day the wind had screamed and the rain had beaten against the windows . . . As evening drew in the storm grew louder and louder, and the wind cried and sobbed like a child in the chimney. Sherlock Holmes sat moodily at one side of the fireplace cross-indexing his records of crime, whilst I at the other was deep in one of Clark Russell's fine sea stories, until the howl of the gale from without seemed to blend with the text, and the splash of the rain to lengthen out into the long swash of the sea waves. My wife was on a visit to her aunt's and for a few days I was a dweller once more in my old quarters at Baker Street."[3]

To the student and the textual critic it is of interest to record that whilst the foregoing quotation is from the accepted version of the Baker Street canon now universally used by biographers and researchers, Watson's original printed account differed in one important particular:

"My wife was on a visit to her *mother's,* [my italics] and for a few days I was a dweller once more in my old quarters in Baker Street."[4]

The proper inference is that Mrs. Watson had both a mother and an aunt in England with whom she used to stay, and that

[1] *The Noble Bachelor,* S., p. 224.

[2] Some experts have suggested that this case occurred after 1889, when Holmes met Irene Adler for the first time, because of his remark to Openshaw, "I have been beaten four times—three times by men and once by a woman". (*The Five Orange Pips,* S., p. 105.) The internal evidence of the Openshaw case apart, this is clearly nonsense. Watson recorded of Irene Adler, with the solemnity of italics, "To Sherlock Holmes she is always *the* woman". (*A Scandal in Bohemia,* S., p. 3.)

[3] *The Five Orange Pips,* S., pp. 103–4.

[4] *The Strand Magazine,* November, 1891, p. 481.

Watson corrected his original slight mistake when he wrote his definitive account.

This remark of Watson's in September, 1887, drives home the certainty that by no stretch of the imagination could this Mrs. Watson conceivably have been Mary Morstan. The latter young lady's statement to Holmes and Watson was clear and precise:

> "My father was an officer in an Indian regiment, who sent me home when I was quite a child. My mother was dead, and I had no relative in England. I was placed, however, in a comfortable boarding establishment at Edinburgh, and there I remained until I was seventeen years of age."[1]

She added that prior to coming to Baker Street, the only people in England to whom she had been able to turn for advice had been the manager of the Langham Hotel, the police and her employer, Mrs. Cecil Forrester.[2]

It is now clear beyond doubt that Watson was married five times; to Constance Adams in 1884 or 1885, to a Miss X, with both a mother and aunt in 1886, to the mother-less and aunt-less Mary Morstan in 1888 or 1889, to a Miss Y. in 1896 and to a Miss Z. in 1902. Miss Dorothy Sayers's challenge in 1949, "Are a fourth and fifth Mrs. Watsons to be disinterred from nameless graves?" has therefore been successfully met by an establishment of the facts, surprising though these may appear to be at first sight. I refer, of course, to the very brief duration of Watson's first two marriages and his fourth. As we have seen, he could not have married Constance Adams earlier than the middle of 1884 and she had clearly been dead for some little time before October, 1886, when we know that he had returned to Baker Street. The marriage to the second Mrs. Watson, from November or December, 1886, to some time late in 1887 or early in 1888, was equally short, and it seems safe to say that Watson's first two wives averaged no more than about eighteen months each. Mary Morstan seems surprisingly to have lasted four or five years, despite her weak heart. The rot set in again with a vengeance, however, with the fourth marriage, for the Mrs. Watson of 1896 seems to have expired before the year

---

[1] *The Sign of Four*, L., p. 153.     [2] *Ibid.*, pp. 153–5.

was out. In a later essay I hope to throw some new light upon the marriage of 1902 and upon the fifth Mrs. Watson, a lady of considerably sterner stuff than her predecessors.

One wonders if invalids and semi-invalids, with short expectations of life, had some curious and possibly perverted attraction for Watson. Such a theory might explain a good deal that is at present obscure, and it can be said that such evidence as is available tends to point in this direction, knowing what we do of the indispositions of Constance Adams and Mary Morstan. A propensity of this kind is by no means unknown to psychologists, and it is important to remember that Watson, as a doctor, would have a natural interest in persons in frail health.

In this connexion it is of interest to recall the possibly parallel case of the poet F. W. H. Myers who, like Holmes, was at Trinity College, Cambridge.[1] Writing a year or two ago in collaboration with my friend Dr. John Lorne Campbell of Canna about some extremely curious goings-on at Ballechin House in Perthshire, between Myers and a young woman whom he took there, Miss Iris Jessica Chaston, I commented upon this lady's reported "weak health". I added:

> "It is odd that at least two other women with whom Myers had associations did not enjoy good health. Mrs. Marshall, the wife of his first cousin, who committed suicide in 1876 after a three-year affair with Myers was "constantly in ill-health", according to Dr. Gauld, as was Mrs. Constance Turner, who died in August, 1890, a matter of four months after her meetings with Myers at Folkestone."[2]

[1] See "A College Friendship?", Hall, pp. 93–108.
[2] J. L. Campbell & T. H. Hall, *Strange Things* (London, 1968), pp. 200–1.

# IV

# SHERLOCK HOLMES AND ANDREW LANG

E XPONENTS of the Higher Criticism of the Baker Street canon have always disagreed with one another. Lord Donegall, reviewing my *Sherlock Holmes, Ten Literary Studies*, wrote:

> "The first objective of every aspiring Higher Critic should be *to prove beyond all reasonable doubt* that every preceding Higher Critic had little idea what he was talking about."[1]

Amiable controversy is an essential ingredient in the great traditions of the literature about the literature of Sherlock Holmes. In my book, after looking back over the years of cheerful and amusing dispute to far away 1929, when *A Note on the Watson Problem* by the late Sir Sydney Roberts, a founding father among Holmesian controversialists, was originally published, I said:[2]

> "This happy thrust and counter-thrust has continued unabated over the years, and I hope therefore that my own entry into the friendly contest of trying to prove that everybody else is wrong, as James Edward Holroyd once described Sherlockian research in a letter to me, will encourage the critics to spring upon me in due course 'like so many staghounds'."[3]

With the traditional background of amiability thus sketched in, it is of interest to consider a contribution to the literature

---

[1] *SHJ*, Winter, 1969, p. 105.  [2] Hall, p. 9.
[3] *A Study in Scarlet*, L., p. 72.

published twelve years ago over the name of the veteran and highly regarded Sherlockian commentator, Thomas S. Blakeney, whose enviable reputation had been permanently established in 1932 by the appearance of his much admired *Sherlock Holmes: Fact or Fiction?*, the first attempt to construct an authentic biography of the great detective.

In 1958 Roger Lancelyn Green, the biographer of Andrew Lang,[1] drew attention to the almost universally forgotten fact that Lang was the first writer to draw attention to some oddities in *The Three Students* and to offer a plausible explanation for them:

> "Scarcely had [*The Three Students*] appeared in the June number of *The Strand Magazine* of 1904 when Andrew Lang —the first critic ever to take the cases of Mr. Sherlock Holmes as the factual reports of Dr. Watson rather than the fictional flings of Dr. Doyle—subjected it to careful analysis in his monthly *causerie* "At the Sign of the Ship" in *Longman's Magazine* (July, 1904), and put forward an interesting theory which no other student seems to have considered.
>
> Lang's contention was that Holmes and Watson were, in this case, made the victims of an elaborate hoax prepared, and brilliantly acted, by Mr. Hilton Soames the tutor, with the aid and connivance of Gilchrist, if not of Bannister the gyp."[2]

The argument was documented by extensive quotation from Lang's original paragraphs about *The Three Students*.[3]

The following issue of *The Sherlock Holmes Journal* contained three letters on the subject, including one from Sir Sydney Roberts:

> "I have been a devotee of Andrew Lang for more than fifty years, but I cannot allow him to be described as 'the first critic ever to take the cases of Mr. Sherlock Holmes as the factual reports of Dr. Watson'. In an 'open letter' to Dr. Watson in *The Cambridge Review* of 23 January, 1902, the late Frank Sidgwick put many searching questions concerning the various dates mentioned in *The Hound of the Baskervilles*.

[1] R. L. Green, *Andrew Lang. A Critical Biography* (Leicester, 1946).
[2] "Dr. Watson's First Critic", *SHJ*, Summer, 1958, pp. 8–9.
[3] *Longman's Magazine*, July, 1904, pp. 269–71.

In fact, I believe that Sidgwick was the first critic to approach the chronological problems round which so much literature has accumulated in later years."[1]

Nathan L. Bengis, an American member of the Sherlock Holmes Society of London, wrote:

"Regarding Roger Lancelyn Green's article, *Dr. Watson's First Critic*, Andrew Lang's article in *Longman's Magazine* for July, 1904, makes out a very plausible theory that Holmes and Watson were the victims of a hoax perpetrated by Hilton Soames and Gilchrist. I was amazed to hear of this, as an almost identical charge was advanced by Vernon Rendall in *The London Nights of Belsize* (London, 1917), Chapter VIII, ('Belsize as a Commentator: Sherlock Holmes'). Mr. Rendall, indeed, went further, and maintained that Dr. Watson was in league with the conspirators 'to give Holmes a job'! What is more, Mr. Rendall's arguments are almost exactly those of Lang!"[2]

The third letter was from Mr. T. S. Blakeney:

"Mr. Roger Lancelyn Green has done us a service by recovering from undeserved obscurity Andrew Lang's criticism of *The Three Students*. He is, however, at fault in saying that no other student has considered the theory put forward by Lang. Ronald Knox criticized certain aspects of *The Three Students* in his *Studies in the Literature of Sherlock Holmes* (1911) and Vernon Rendall did so in a chapter in *The London Nights of Belsize* (1917)—both of these recently reprinted in *The Incunabular [Sherlock] Holmes*. Sir Sydney Roberts referred briefly to Rendall's theory as 'interesting, though not wholly convincing' (*A Note on the Watson Problem*) and I may add that I discussed those views in some detail in my own book, and am still of opinion that, for the reasons I gave, it is sounder to accept the tale as a true one, despite some inconsistences in it, than to treat it as a 'frame-up' on Holmes. Vernon Rendall, however, in his essay, 'The Limitations of Sherlock Holmes' in *Baker Street Studies* (1934) disposed of my rejoinders by the simple process of ignoring them, merely reiterating his earlier

---

[1] *The SHJ*, Winter, 1958, p. 24.
[2] *Ibid.*, pp. 25.

view. His faulty judgments in this later essay, however, undermine Rendall's standing as a serious critic.

What seems to me of special interest in Mr. Green's article is that Vernon Rendall was anticipated by Lang to such a degree that I find myself wondering whether there is not a suggestion of plagiarism in Rendall's essay. Did he know of Lang's essay of thirteen years before, and did he hope that it had escaped notice—as indeed it has done till now?"[1]

There can be no doubt, I fancy, about Blakeney's annoyance with Rendall. The implication that the latter had copied from Lang was plain. Coupled as this was with the suggestion that Rendall might have hoped that Lang's essay of 1904 had escaped notice, it is clear that Blakeney was making a severe criticism of Rendall in complete contrast with the friendly leg-pulling which had typified most previous Sherlockian controversy.

Vernon Horace Rendall (1869–1960) was a formidable literary figure and a member of a brilliant family. His brother, Dr. Montague John Rendall, C.M.G., was the Headmaster of Winchester. A Major Scholar of Trinity College, Cambridge, in 1889, Vernon Rendall was included in the first-class list of the Classical Tripos in 1891. Among other appointments of distinction he became the Editor of both the *Athenaeum* and *Notes and Queries*, and Literary Editor of the *English Review*. His published works included *The Profitable Imbroglio*, 1910, *The London Nights of Belsize*, 1917, *Hallowmead, Ltd*, 1927, *Wild Flowers in Literature*, 1934 and *Anthology of Courtship and Wooing*, 1936. He received a Civil List pension in 1937. His contributions to the literature of Sherlock Holmes consisted of the chapter in *The London Nights of Belsize* at which Blakeney's main criticism of plagiarism was directed, and a later essay "The Limitations of Sherlock Holmes", published in 1934 in *Baker Street Studies*, edited by H. W. Bell, of which Blakeney said, as we have seen, that the faulty judgments in it undermined Rendall's reputation as a serious critic.

In his book in 1932 Blakeney had devoted six pages to the refutation of Rendall's hypothesis in regard to *The Three Students*,[2] of which I quote the beginning and the end:

[1] *The SHJ*, Winter, 1958, pp. 24–5.
[2] Blakeney, pp. 91–6.

"[Rendall] boldly claims that Watson deliberately hood-winked Holmes in the affair of the Three Students, with the aid of Soames, Gilchrist and Bannister. Holmes, it is suggested, was worried over his charters, and to prevent his finding solace in drugs, Watson arranged a spoof job for him to investigate . . . Having regard to the rejoinders we have entered to Mr. Rendall's other points, and looking to the character of Watson as we know it, we confess we find it more difficult to believe in the hypothesis that the case of *The Three Students* was a 'frame up' than in the canonicity of the events described, possible inconsistencies in the narrative notwithstanding."

This was both courteous and mild, and was consistent with the established friendly tone of the previously published work of other Higher Critics. It was perfectly true that in 1934 Rendall had ignored all that Blakeney had said about *The Three Students* two years earlier. He wrote:

"The story of *The Three Students* contains deductions founded on supposed facts which to a classical scholar are ridiculous. I have suggested elsewhere that this case is really Watson's masterpiece, got up to keep Holmes amused when he was feeling the lack of his home and his usual occupations."[1]

Rendall's only mention of Blakeney's book occurred in a long footnote, and was a criticism of a phrase of the latter's which could be read as implying that Jean Paul and Richter were different persons. Rendall wrote:

"In this connection, it is strange that Mr. T. S. Blakeney (*Sherlock Holmes; Fact or Fiction?* p. 14) should regard 'Jean Paul' and 'Richter', mentioned on the same page, as different persons. Watson got at Jean Paul through Carlyle, and Mr. Blakeney might, with a minimum of trouble, have perceived that both references are to the same man. Richter explains in his unfinished *Autobiography*, which is available in English, the original of his two names, John Paul, and promises to tell his readers why he adopted 'Jean Paul' as a pen-name, first used in his *Unsichtbare Loge*. He did not give the promised explanation; but, as Ernst Förster suggests in the biography attached to Vol. XVI of the *Collected Works*

---

[1] *Baker Street Studies*, pp. 74–5.

in German, the pen-name was doubtless intended as a tribute to the French culture from which he had learnt so much."[1]

It may be thought that this display of literary expertise[2] in the faintly scornful reference to Blakeney's mistake,[3] coupled with Rendall's contemptuous dismissal of the "deductions founded on supposed facts" contained in *The Three Students* (which Blakeney had defended) "which to a classical scholar are ridiculous", would not please the latter writer.

However that may be, I think that our first judgment must be that Rendall undoubtedly initiated the disagreement in 1934 by criticising Blakeney in unnecessarily lofty and provocative terms, and that Blakeney had reason to be offended. It therefore seems probable and natural that Green's revelation in 1958 of Lang's early criticism of *The Three Students*, previously unknown to most Sherlockians, would be of special interest to Blakeney. Whether the substance of his comments on Rendall was justified, however, is a matter which can only be determined by looking at the facts. Lang wrote in 1904:

"I have often thought that Dr. Watson overrates the acuteness of his friend and hero, Sherlock Holmes. In some cases Sherlock has blundered egregiously, and been taken in, though he never knew it. Now, in the *Strand* for June, Sherlock is the victim of a college don and an undergraduate, who have 'played it rather low' on the world-famed detective.

Sherlock was at Oxford or Cambridge, studying 'early English charters', couched, probably, in the Latin language. Soames of St. Luke's came to him with a cock-and-bull story, which would not have taken in a Fifth Form boy. According to Soames, the tutor, who proved too hard for Holmes, he was one of the examiners for the Fortescue Scholarship— whether a University scholarship or an in-college affair does not appear, but it was for senior men. The first paper

---

[1] *Baker Street Studies*, p. 74, n. 3.

[2] It is interesting, in this connexion, to see that Rendall copied *verbatim* and without comment Holmes's unfortunate misquotation of Flaubert, "L'homme c'est rien—l'oeuvre c'est tout", on p. 83 of *Baker Street Studies*. (*The Red-Headed League*, S., p. 55 and, for the correction, Hall, p. 49).

[3] Rendall's work was not free from this human frailty. On p. 74 of *Baker Street Studies*, for example, he wrote that Holmes "refers to Horace (*A Case of Identity*, I, 75) and quotes him (*A Study in Scarlet*, II, 139)". A glance at the latter reference, however, shows that it was Watson who advised Holmes to content himself with the consciousness of success, and quoted Horace in so doing.

was to be Greek 'unseen', 'a large passage of Greek transla-
tion which the candidate has not seen'. Now, it is never easy to
know what candidates have *not* seen, and a chunk of Helio-
dorus might do, with a bit of the *Cassandra* of Lycophron, and
perhaps a corrupt little piece out of Herodas, if he spells his
name in that way.

But Soames, guying the innocent Holmes, actually persuaded him that, by way of unseen, he was setting 'half a
chapter of Thucydides'. Naturally every man who went in
(they were not schoolboys, but senior men) had read the
whole of Thucydides. To set the Halimusian for unseen
would be the act of an idiot. Next, the passage was so long
that, though only half a chapter of the history which the son
of Olorus compiled, it covered 'three long slips' of printers'
proofs. No chapter, no *whole* chapter in 'Thicksides' is as
long as that, I think; certainly no half-chapter is. They are
quite 'snappy little pars.', many of them—the chapters in
Thucydides.

But Sherlock sucked it all in. He believed that a bad young
man, wanting to get up unseen Thucydides, would be such
an inconceivable donkey as to begin copying it out in pencil.
Of course, even if he had not read all Thucydides, he would
merely glance at it, and see what book the extract came from.
Nobody who goes in for a scholarship for senior men could
make such an error. However ignorant he was, the first line
would suffice for his wicked purpose. He could compare it
with the beginnings of chapters, but, if he knew no more than
to be in doubt, he could not have got the Fortescue Scholarship. But Soames palmed all this series of transparent hoaxes
off upon Holmes—every step in the series an obvious 'sell'—
and so Holmes went about to catch the culprit. One of the
men was in the joke with Soames; he was one of the three
on the tutor's stair, and confessed to having surreptitiously
copied a huge cantle of a half-chapter of Thucydides in pencil,
from the proof-sheet of the examination-paper, and the same
with intent to deceive.

'Well, Soames, we have cleared your little problem up',
said Sherlock with his usual complacency, and when he had
left the tutor's rooms that grave man threw off his dignity,
and waltzed with his undergraduate accomplice round the
table. For not one of the incidents could have occurred.
Thucydides could not, I hope, have been set for unseen in

PLATE V. Professor Moriarty
(*see p.* 104)

PLATE VI. Holmes, Watson and Mycroft Holmes
(*see p.* 110)

such an examination. A half-chapter of Thucydides could not be as long as three examination-papers. A dishonest man would not have needed to copy more than a line, if he copied any of it. Soames, in the circumstances, would have substituted any other paper for the first, and set new pieces of unseen; not one monstrous slice of one author. What Sherlock Holmes will say to Dr. Watson for thus exposing him I know not, and Watson would have done better to keep the whole story in reserve, as giving him a hold over Holmes, when next he was bumptious—his besetting sin. That a don and an undergraduate took in Holmes by means so simple and so audacious is rather a comfort to a less successful explorer of mysteries (historical). Literature triumphed over Science, for once in a way. *Non omnia possumus omnes*, as Partridge said; we all have our moments of weakness. If Holmes had asked Soames to show him that half-chapter in the original, Soames would have been exposed himself.

Let me not be supposed to depreciate the great qualities of Sherlock. If an adventure of his appeared every day, it would find in me a happy reader. The mistakes may be Dr. Watson's, and the unseens may have been unseens that could be set in the Fortescue Scholarship. Probably they are best selected out of things like Plato, his *Laws*, or Callimachus, or Polybius, or other authors whom few undergraduates have read exhaustively."[1]

In 1912, in *The Oxford Blue Book*, Monsignor Ronald A. Knox first published his "Studies in the Literature of Sherlock Holmes", which was afterwards reprinted in *Essays in Satire* (London, 1928). One paragraph was devoted to *The Three Students*:

"Is it likely that a University scholarship paper—nay, an Oxford scholarship paper, for the Quadrangle is mentioned in connexion with it—should be printed only one day before the examination? That it should consist of only half a chapter of Thucydides? That this half-chapter should take the examiner an hour and a half to correct for the press? That the proofs of the half-chapter should be in three consecutive slips? Moreover, if a pencil was marked with the name Johann Faber, how could the two letters NN, and these two only, be left on the stump?"[2]

[1] *Longman's Magazine*, July, 1904, pp. 269–71.    [2] *Essays in Satire*, p. 152.

It is clear that Knox did not copy from Lang, for not one of the five oddities remarked upon by him coincided with the points made by Lang, unless it be urged that the slightly obscure phrase in regard to the unlikelihood of the proofs of the half-chapter being in three consecutive slips was intended to mean, as Lang had observed, that no half-chapter of Thucydides was long enough to cover three slips of printer's proofs. It may be thought that any suggestion of plagiarism which relied upon such tenuous evidence as this must fail.

Five years later Rendall's commentary on *The Three Students* was published.[1] The relevant sentences are:

"In the first place, there is no whole chapter in Thucydides which would occupy anything like as much as three slips of ordinary or special proof matter. Any one tolerably familiar both with Thucydides and printing could have told Mr. Holmes as much off-hand. In the second place, Soames could not possibly have spent as much as an hour and a half in reading the proofs through, and he did not even finish them in that time! Greek, being unlike Latin, widely divergent from English, is recognized by printers as a language requiring special care, and generally well set up. University printers at least would make few mistakes in such 'copy', and it is ludicrous to suppose that an examiner for a University scholarship, well up in his Greek, would occupy more than half the supposed time in making corrections . . . Whatever the passage set was, from Thucydides or another, any student of sufficient knowledge and practice in Greek to enter for a University scholarship would take about a minute to get a clue to its authorship in the dangerous room, without throwing the proofs about, and would then leave to complete his researches in his own room, or in some library, perhaps the very library where Holmes was poring over early English charters. He would see that the passage was continuous, and would simply memorize one or possibly two rare words (sure to occur in an unseen set in a University scholarship), look them up in Liddell and Scott (a Greek Lexicon, Mr. Holmes) at ease, and so get the exact reference, which would enable him to study the passage set at his ease with the aid of a commentator or translator . . ."

[1] "Belsize as a Commentator: Sherlock Holmes", *The London Nights of Belsize* (London, 1917), pp. 147–57.

It will be seen at once that Rendall drew attention to three principal inconsistencies, of which the first and the third were that the unseen from Thucydides could not have occupied three slips of proof, and that the student intent on cheating would not have needed to copy out the half-chapter, but would only have required to identify it in order to study the original source in private. Lang, it will be recalled, had made both these points in 1904:

"Though only half a chapter of the history which the son of Olorus compiled, it covered 'three long slips' of printers' proofs. No chapter, no *whole* chapter in 'Thicksides' is as long as that, I think; certainly no half-chapter is."

"He would merely glance at it, and see what book the extract came from . . . A dishonest man would not have needed to copy more than a line, if he copied any of it."

A significant point of detail is that the unseen was, of course, described in *The Three Students* in no other way but as "half a chapter of Thucydides". It was Lang who had emphasised the shortness of such an extract and the consequent impossibility of it occupying three slips of proof, by asserting that "no chapter, no *whole* chapter in 'Thicksides' is as long as that, I think". Rendall's sentence on this subject is therefore worthy of particular scrutiny:

"In the first place, there is no whole chapter in Thucydides which would occupy anything like as much as three slips of ordinary or special proof matter."

We are entitled to speculate upon the provenance of Rendall's use of the precise phrase used by Lang, "no whole chapter", knowing as we do that there was nothing in the text of *The Three Students* to suggest it.

Rendall's second point of alleged inconsistency in *The Three Students* was that "Soames could not possibly have spent as much as an hour and a half in reading the proofs through". Lang made no suggestion of this kind. We cannot avoid noticing, however, that one of the oddities listed by Ronald Knox five years previously in the form of questions had been "Is it likely

. . . that this half-chapter should take the examiner an hour and a half to correct for the press?"

These disconcerting matters of detail apart, we cannot set on one side the fact that the whole essence of Lang's essay in 1904 was that the case of *The Three Students* was a hoax. Holmes had been the "victim of a college don [Soames] and an undergraduate [Gilchrist]", and had "been taken in, although he never knew it". The sum and substance of Rendall's "Belsize as a Commentator: Sherlock Holmes" was similar. He admittedly increased the number of hoaxers to four, identifying them as Watson, Soames, Gilchrist and Bannister [a college servant], and gave them a definite motive for the deceiving of Holmes as opposed to the mere "joke" postulated by Lang. Can we now seriously doubt, however, the source of the original idea? Rendall wrote:

"[Gilchrist], Soames and the servant were in league with Watson to give Holmes a job. Holmes was uncomfortable over his charters, and in a bad temper. He needed work more exciting. Watson feared his relapse into the drug-habit (this fear is openly expressed in the Cambridge story in the same series, 'The Adventure of the Missing Three-Quarter') and Watson got up this pretty little case for him. The stage managing was quite creditable; in fact, this is Watson's masterpiece, though I do not think he realized the full absurdity of the supposed proceedings."

Not the least damning point in the case for Rendall's plagiarism is his account of the pleasure expressed by the hoaxers at their success as soon as Holmes had gone, "particularly cheered, no doubt, by the edifying little exhortation he delivered to the culprit". Rendall continued:

"When [Holmes and Watson] had left, the young man burst into a hearty laugh. Soames smiled, and merely said, 'Bannister,[1] I thought you had overdone it. That fit of yours in the chair, you know. It was temerarious'."

It is difficult not to suspect that the inspiration for this scene did not owe something to Lang's essay:

[1] Bannister was the elderly college servant. The undergraduate, or "young man", was Gilchrist.

" 'Well, Soames, we have cleared your little problem up', said Sherlock with his usual complacency, and when he had left the tutor's rooms that grave man threw off his dignity and waltzed with his undergraduate accomplice round the table. For not one of the incidents could have occurred."

There can be no doubt that Blakeney's most serious criticism of Rendall was the second phrase of the sentence:

"Did he know of Lang's essay of thirteen years before, and did he hope that it had escaped notice—as indeed it has done till now?"

It must be said at once, I think, that in 1904 Rendall was the Editor of both the *Athenaeum* and *Notes and Queries*, and that it is therefore reasonable to suppose that in his special position in the literary scene he would probably be familiar with Lang's contributions to *Longman's Magazine* at the time. Can it equally be said, however, that in 1917 Rendall might have thought that after thirteen years those few paragraphs would have sunk into comfortable and safe obscurity so far as most people were concerned? It is interesting in this connexion to recall that both Blakeney and Bengis, despite their special interest in everything connected with Sherlock Holmes, confessed that Lang's contribution to the literature of Baker Street was unknown to them until R. L. Green's essay appeared. It is of equal importance to consider the case of one of the leading authorities on the literature of Sherlock Holmes, the late Edgar W. Smith, which could scarcely be more apposite. I am happy to have this opportunity of mentioning his work, which is now most difficult to obtain, and recording my admiration of it.

In 1958 *The Incunabular Sherlock Holmes*, edited by Smith, was published in Morristown, New Jersey, by the Baker Street Irregulars Incorporated, in a limited edition of three hundred and fifty copies. Its stated purpose was to bring together in chronological order the shorter works, mainly in periodicals, of the early commentators on the Baker Street canon. As the Editor wrote in his Foreword, most of these essays were "hard to find in their original appearances, or even in the form of available reprints", and it had therefore seemed to him

appropriate and desirable to publish this "retrospective Sherlockian reader, so that we may cogitate upon what is old under
the sun, and match our own qualities and our own achievements
with those of the pioneers". Although Smith's collection was in
chronological order through the first third of the twentieth
century, commencing with two pieces of editorial comment on
Sherlock Holmes by Arthur Bartlett in *The Bookman* and Frank
Sidgwick's "An Open Letter to Dr. Watson" about *The Hound
of the Baskervilles* in the *Cambridge Review*, all printed in 1902,
the Editor was entirely silent about Andrew Lang's published
contributions to the literature. It is not unreasonable to say that
if so well-informed an authority as Edgar W. Smith was not
aware that Andrew Lang had written about Sherlock Holmes,
twice in 1904 and once in 1905, the case for Lang's contributions
to the literature of Baker Street having been lost in almost
absolute obscurity is greatly strengthened.

I hope that I have been able to throw some light on this old
controversy. The facts seem to me strongly to suggest that
Blakeney's criticism of Rendall was well-founded, although the
implication that it was only Lang's work of which unacknow-
ledged use was made was not entirely correct, as we have seen
from the examination of Knox's "Studies in the Literature of
Sherlock Holmes". I am not aware that Rendall, who was
89 in 1958, ever replied to Blakeney's strictures, but I do not
think that any significance need be attached to this. Rendall was
not a member of the Sherlock Holmes Society and may never
have seen the relevant issue of the *Journal*.

It was entirely natural for Andrew Lang to be interested in
Sherlock Holmes and to write about him. His biographer says
of him, "For mystery novels Lang always had a weakness, and
in a later age he was one of the first to welcome the advent of
Sherlock Holmes".[1] In 1904, the year that has been relevant to
this inquiry, his book *Historical Mysteries* was published. Green
says of it, "Lang ranges from Gowrie to the Chevalier D'Eon,
and from Sir Edmund Berry Godfrey to the Cardinal's Necklace.
These mysteries are among the most readable of Lang's
historical works, and do at times approach very near to the
excitement of an ordinary detective story."[2]

[1] Green, *op. cit.*, p. 162.                [2] *Ibid.*, p. 199.

*The Incunabular Sherlock Holmes* did not include five pleasant pages about Holmes and Watson contributed by Lang to *The Quarterly Review* in July, 1904. Included in a longer essay on Conan Doyle, these paragraphs offered character studies of the great detective and his Boswell, and compared Holmes with Dupin to the advantage of the former. In the same place, Lang first drew attention to Holmes's apparent ignorance of "the ordinary British system of titles":

> "He has a client, and he looks for that client in another 'book of reference', not the light-hearted gazetteer which he consults with the pious confidence that Mrs. Gallup bestows on the 'Encyclopaedia Britannica'. He discovers that the client's name is 'Lord Robert Walsingham de Vere St. Simon, second son of the Duke of Balmoral'—not a plausible title at best. Yet, knowing this, and finding, in the 'Morning Post', the client's real name, both Sherlock and the egregious Watson speak of Lord Robert St Simon throughout as 'Lord St Simon'! The unhappy 'nobleman', with equal ignorance of his place in life, signs himself, 'Yours faithfully, St. Simon'.
>
> Of course we expect that so clumsy a pretender to be the second son of a duke will be instantly exposed by the astute Sherlock. Not so; Sherlock 'thinks it all very capital'. Now would Sherlock have called the late Lord Randolph Churchill 'Lord Churchill', or would he have been surprised to hear that Lord Randolph did not sign himself 'Churchill'? Anthropology we do not expect from Sherlock, but he really ought to have known matters of everyday usage. The very 'page boy' announces 'Lord Robert St Simon'; but Sherlock salutes the visitor as 'Lord St Simon', and the pretended nobleman calls his wife 'Lady St Simon'. But do not let us be severe on the great detective for knowing no more of anthropology than of other things! Rather let us wish him 'good hunting', and prepare to accompany Dr. Watson and him, when next they load their revolvers, and go forth to the achieving of great adventures."[1]

Lang's reference to "the light-hearted gazetteer" and to Holmes's lack of knowledge of anthropology in this amusing criticism were in regard to some earlier paragraphs in the same essay in which he took Holmes to task over his identification of

[1] *The Quarterly Review*, July, 1904, p. 179.

Tonga, "the unhallowed dwarf with his hideous face", of *The Sign of Four*, as an Andaman islander:

"The Andamanese are cruelly libelled, and have neither the malignant qualities, nor the heads like mops, nor the weapons, nor the customs, with which they are credited by Sherlock. He has detected the wrong savage, and injured the character of an amiable people. The *bö: jig-ngijji* is really a religious, kindly creature, has a Deluge and a Creation myth, and shaves his head, not possessing scissors. Sherlock confessedly took his knowledge of the *bö: jig-ngijji* from 'a gazetteer', which is full of nonsense. 'The average height is below four feet'! The average height is four feet ten inches and a half. The gazetteer says that 'massacres are invariably concluded by a cannibal feast'. Mr. E. H. Man, who knows the people thoroughly, says 'no lengthened investigation was needed to disprove this long-credited fiction, for not a trace could be discovered of the existence of such a practice in their midst, ever in far-off times.'

In short, if Mr. Sherlock Holmes, instead of turning up a common work of reference, had merely glanced at the photographs of Andamanese, trim, elegant, closely-shaven men, and a few pages in Mr. Man's account of them in 'The Journal of the Anthropological Institute' for 1881, he would have sought elsewhere for his little savage villain with the blow-pipe. A Fuegian who had lived a good deal on the Amazon might have served his turn.

A man like Sherlock, who wrote a monograph on over a hundred varieties of tobacco-ash, ought not to have been gulled by a gazetteer. Sherlock's Andamanese fights with a blow-pipe and poisoned arrows. Neither poisoned arrows nor blow-pipes are used by the islanders, according to Mr. Man. These melancholy facts demonstrate that Mr. Holmes was not the paragon of Dr. Watson's fond imagination."[1]

Lang's light-hearted and charming style made him an ideal exponent of the Higher Criticism as applied to the literature of Sherlock Holmes, and it is a privilege to have this opportunity of preserving these fragments in permanent form, and thus repairing their omission from *The Incunabular Sherlock Holmes*. Lang's a most important contribution to the subject, however

[1] *The Quarterly Review, op. cit.*, pp. 178–9.

(and so far as I know, his third and last), was his creation of a miniature Baker Street story in which Holmes applied his analytical skill to the problems raised by Dickens's *The Mystery of Edwin Drood*. In view of its length, however, I must refer the interested reader to pp. 473–80 of *Longman's Magazine*, September, 1905.

# V

# DR. WATSON AND
# THE ENGLISH COUNTIES

S IR SYDNEY ROBERTS suggested that Watson "was most fully at home in the sheltering arms of the great metropolis: Baker Street, the Underground, hansom cabs, Turkish baths, November fogs—these, it would seem, are of the very stuff of Watson's life".[1] Watson himself, on the other hand, described London as "that great cesspool into which all the loungers and idlers of the Empire are irresistibly drained".[2]

In my earlier book I offered the opinion that Watson was a Hampshire man, on the firm basis of the text of the canon. We recall that during a hot August day in London, he "yearned for the glades of the New Forest or the shingle of Southsea".[3] During a train journey to Winchester (which with admirable loyalty to his native county he described as "the old English capital") on "an ideal spring day" with "a light blue sky, flecked with fleecy white clouds drifting across from west to east", Watson became lyrical over the beauty of the countryside around Aldershot, with its rolling hills, farmhouses and the light green of the fresh foliage.[4] In another context, and at a different time of the year, he enthused over the "wonderful autumnal panorama" of the Hampshire rural scene.[5]

We know, of course, that Watson spent part of his youth in Australia,[6] and was educated at one of England's great public schools in company with his friend Percy (Tadpole) Phelps,

---

[1] Roberts, p. 62.
[2] *A Study in Scarlet*, L., p. 6.
[3] *The Cardboard Box*, S., p. 924.
[4] *The Copper Beeches*, S., p. 285.
[5] *Thor Bridge*, S., p. 1240.
[6] *The Sign of Four*, L., p. 178.

the "extremely well-connected" nephew of Lord Holdhurst.[1] Watson perforce lived in London whilst reading for his medical degree and ultimately obtaining the coveted M.D. of the University of London,[2] but he returned to Hampshire to the great military hospital, built originally for the wounded in the Crimean War, on Southampton Water at Netley. There he took the prescribed course for army surgeons, and his disastrous military career of approximately one year followed. Wounded at the battle of Maiwand and struck down by enteric fever whilst at the base hospital at Peshawur, he returned to England as a convalescent.

Watson himself said that he "naturally gravitated to London", where he led "a comfortless, meaningless existence"[3] until he met Holmes and the wonderful years of partnership in Baker Street began. It was then, and only then, it may be thought, that his life in London became attractive to him. It follows, I fancy, that Sir Sydney's suggestion that Watson was "most fully at home in the sheltering arms of the great metropolis" must rely upon the presence of Sherlock Holmes rather than upon the November fogs. Watson's pleasure in living with Holmes in Baker Street is thoroughly understandable, but it need not blind us to the fact that if the great detective could have conducted his practice from a Hampshire village, Watson would have enjoyed their association even more.

Watson was the most typical of Englishmen, and there is ample evidence in the canon to show that whilst his praise of Hampshire was, of course, paramount, he delighted in the beauties of his native country as a whole. He much admired, for example, the scenery of Surrey, for we notice that in the sinister affair at Stoke Moran, Watson described "the lovely Surrey lanes", where "the trees and wayside hedges were just throwing out their first green shoots, and the air was full of the pleasant smell of the moist earth".[4] He was attracted by "the

---

[1] *The Naval Treaty*, S., p. 499. Dr. W. S. Bristowe has suggested that the school was probably Wellington, (*SHJ*, December, 1954, pp. 32–3) on the reasonable conjecture that its strong army influence may have been an ingredient in Watson's ultimate decision to join the Services and that as Watson later played for Blackheath (*The Sussex Vampire*, S., p. 1182) it is probable that he attended one of the few schools where Rugby football was favoured in those days.

[2] *A Study in Scarlet*, L., p. 5.          [3] *Ibid.*, p. 6.
[4] *The Speckled Band*, S., p. 187.

fir-woods and heather of Woking",[1] the home of his unfortunate friend Percy Phelps, whilst the neighbourhood of Charlington Hall, "near Farnham, on the borders of Surrey",[2] was remembered by Watson as a "heath covered with golden patches of flowering gorse, gleaming magnificently in the light of the bright spring sunshine".[3] Despite the discomforts of the visit to Wisteria Lodge, on "a cold, dark March evening, with a sharp wind and a fine rain beating upon our faces", Watson was uninfluenced by the weather conditions and described the location of the case of Mr. John Scott Eccles as "the pretty Surrey village of Esher".[4]

The murder of Sir Eustace Brackenstall took Holmes and Watson to Marsham in Kent "on a bitterly cold and frosty morning during the winter of '97", leaving behind them what Watson described (significantly, we may think) as "the opalescent London reek".[5] Despite the weather and the horrific features of the case, however, Watson did not fail to notice with appreciation that "the avenue ran through a noble park, between lines of ancient elms".[6] Similarly, during the journey to Herefordshire to save James McCarthy from the hangman, Watson obviously enjoyed "passing through the beautiful Stroud valley and over the broad gleaming Severn", and his stay at the Hereford Arms in "'the pretty little country town of Ross".[7]

Sussex, because of its proximity to Watson's own Hampshire, obviously had special attractions for him. It is not surprising, therefore, that he enthused when at Birlstone over "the quaint village street with a row of pollarded elms on either side of it", and recorded that the winding drive of the old Manor House had "such sward and oaks around it as one only sees in rural England". He found time, moreover, amid the "grim and terrible intrigue" of the case, to admire "the beautiful broad moat, as still and luminous as quicksilver in the cold winter sunshine".[8] When Holmes and he were at Woodman's Lee, near Forest Row, looking into the death of Captain Peter Carey, killed with his own harpoon and "pinned like a beetle to a card",[9] Watson

---

[1] *The Naval Treaty*, S., p. 501.   [2] *The Solitary Cyclist*, S., p. 640.
[3] *Ibid.*, p. 646.   [4] *Wisteria Lodge*, S., p. 904.   [5] *The Abbey Grange*, S., p. 833.
[6] *Ibid.*, p. 835.   [7] *The Boscombe Valley Mystery*, S., p. 84.
[8] *The Valley of Fear*, L., p. 493.   [9] *Black Peter*, S., p. 702.

was only too happy, during an interval in the investigation, to go for a walk in the "beautiful woods" around Forest Row, and to "give a few hours to the birds and the flowers".[1]

Watson's affection for the English scene was not confined to the gentle, green landscapes of which some examples have been assembled. He found "the cold, bracing atmosphere of the Peak country, in which Dr. Huxtable's famous school is situated",[2] very much to his liking, despite the loneliness of "the great rolling moor", uninhabited other than by the plover and the curlew.[3] During one of his visits to Dartmoor he described "the glories of the landscape", and in particular the sunset behind the stables at Capleton, causing the moor to be "tinged with gold, deepening into rich, ruddy brown where the faded ferns and brambles caught the evening light".[4] Dartmoor clearly fascinated Watson, for during a longer stay there, whilst exulting in "the fresh beauty" of his first morning at Baskerville Hall, he still recalled the "grey, melancholy hill, with a strange jagged summit, dim and vague in the distance, like some fantastic landscape in a dream",[5] which had been his first glimpse of the moor during the previous evening. He had observed with keen appreciation how the "rolling pasture lands curved upwards on either side of us, and old gabled houses peeped out from the thick green foliage", but the impression had remained with him that "behind the peaceful and sunlit countryside there rose ever dark against the evening sky, the long, gloomy curve of the moor, broken by the jagged and sinister hills".[6] Watson's reaction to the scenery and atmosphere of neighbouring Cornwall was very similar. He described it as "a country of rolling moors, lonely and dun-coloured, with an occasional church tower to mark the site of some old-world village", and it is clear that "the glamour and mystery of the place" had great attraction for him.[7] Possibly influenced subconsciously by the fact that the Cornish peninsula, upon which the cottage rented by Holmes and Watson stood, was the scene of "the Cornish horror", however, he found that the sea view of Mounts Bay gave him a sense of unease, and he described it as "that old death trap of

[1] *Black Peter*, p. 707.   [2] *The Priory School*, S., p. 669.   [3] *Ibid.*, p. 674.
[4] *Silver Blaze*, S., p. 320.   [5] *The Hound of the Baskervilles*, L., p. 329.
[6] *Ibid.*, p. 330.   [7] *The Devil's Foot*, S., p. 1042.

sailing vessels, with its fringe of black cliffs and surge-swept reefs in which innumerable seamen have met their end."[1]

It has been said that there is no more typical part of rural England than the remote and historic lands of East Anglia. Watson recorded for us his own impression of the eastern counties during the visit by Holmes and himself to Ridling Thorpe Manor in Norfolk, the home of Mr. Hilton Cubitt. Mr. Cubitt had already visited Baker Street, and, in Watson's words, "seemed to bring a whiff of his strong, fresh, bracing, east-coast air with him". Was there a note of envy in Watson's remark, possibly a significant one in the present context, that Mr. Cubitt's "clear eyes and florid cheeks told of a life led far from the fogs of Baker Street"?[2] It is noteworthy that during the seven-mile drive from North Walsham, whilst Holmes was "lost in gloomy speculation", Watson found much to interest and delight him in the countryside, "where a few scattered cottages represented the population of today, while on every hand enormous square-towered churches bristled up from the flat, green landscape and told of the glory and prosperity of old East Anglia".[3] It was only as "the violet rim of the German ocean appeared over the green edge of the Norfolk coast" that the carriage came within sight of Ridling Thorpe Manor,[4] where they were to find that Hilton Cubitt had been killed during the small hours.

The general submission contained in this essay would seem to be supported by the fact that whilst Watson obviously delighted in the English rural scene, he had little or nothing to tell us about the towns to which the cases sometimes took the two friends. In the matter of the Franco-Midland Hardware Company, for example, Watson's reference to Birmingham was limited to the brief and factual information that he and Holmes walked down Corporation Street.[5] The single exception is Cambridge, but Cambridge is no ordinary town. Although he was not educated there, Watson clearly enjoyed the beauty of the "ancient colleges"[6] and in particular "the ancient lichen-tinted court of the old college" of St. Luke's.[7] At the crisis of

---

[1] *The Devil's Foot*, S., p. 1041.  [2] *The Dancing Men*, S., p. 612.
[3] *Ibid.*, pp. 622–3.  [4] *Ibid.*, p. 623.  [5] *The Stockbroker's Clerk*, S., p. 366.
[6] *The Creeping Man*, S., p. 1254.  [7] *The Three Students*, S., p. 767.

the affair of Professor Presbury, when Holmes and Watson were hiding in the bushes of the famous physiologist's garden, Watson found time to observe the clouds scudding across the Cambridge night sky, "obscuring from time to time the half-moon".[1]

Enough evidence has been assembled, I fancy, to dispose of Sir Sydney Roberts's suggestion that Watson was only truly content in London. That much of his life was spent there is not in dispute, but he was not a Londoner either by birth or inclination. He endured, like the old campaigner he was, "the greasy, heavy brown swirl" of the November fogs,[2] and the blazing hot days in August when "Baker Street was like an oven, and the glare of the sunlight upon the yellow brickwork of the house across the road was painful to the eye",[3] for only one reason. To our everlasting advantage and pleasure he discovered in 1881 that his vocation in life was to be that of the partner and biographer of Sherlock Holmes of Baker Street.

[1] *The Creeping Man*, S., p. 1261.
[2] *The Bruce-Partington Plans*, S., p. 968.
[3] *The Cardboard Box.*, S., pp. 923–4.

# VI

## THE PROBLEM
## OF THE UNPUBLISHED CASES

IN 1954 *The Exploits of Sherlock Holmes* was published by John Murray. The collaborating authors were Mr. Adrian Conan Doyle and Mr. John Dickson Carr, respectively the son and the authorised biographer of Dr. Watson's literary agent. The book, our first fresh glimpse of Baker Street for over a quarter of a century, was received with enthusiasm by Sherlockians all over the world. Of its twelve stories, eleven concerned themselves with some of those cases to which Dr. Watson had made brief but tantalising reference in the published literature, without any details. I have not been able to trace any mention by Watson in the canon of the affair of Madame Taupin's wax-works, which the authors of *The Exploits* called "The Adventures of the Wax Gamblers".

To the Baker Street student it was of the greatest interest to have available for the first time these reconstructions of some of the cases to which Watson had referred in merely a phrase or a sentence. The eleven stories in this category published in *The Exploits* were those of "The Seven Clocks" or "the case of the Trepoff murder",[1] "The Gold Hunter" or "the Camberwell poisoning case",[2] "The Highgate Miracle" or "Mr. James Phillimore, who, stepping back into his own house to get his umbrella, was never more seen in this world",[3] "The Black Baronet" or "the unfortunate Mme. Montpensier",[4] "The Sealed Room" or "Colonel Warburton's madness",[5] "Foulkes

---

[1] *A Scandal in Bohemia*, S., p. 4.   [2] *The Five Orange Pips*, S., p. 103.
[3] *Thor Bridge*, S., p. 1215.   [4] *The Hound of the Baskervilles*, L., p. 443.
[5] *The Engineer's Thumb*, S., p. 201.

Rath" or "the Addleton tragedy",[1] "The Abbas Ruby" or "the famous card scandal of the Nonpareil Club",[2] "The Two Women" or the blackmailing case involving "one of the most revered names in England",[3] "The Dark Angels" or "the Ferrers Documents",[4] "The Deptford Horror" or "Wilson, the notorious canary-trainer"[5] and "The Red Widow" or "the Arnsworth Castle business".[6] It was clear from the text that all this had been made possible because some of Watson's notes and literary remains had come into the possession of the authors.

*The Exploits of Sherlock Holmes* was immensely popular, proceeding successfully through several hard-back issues to a paper-back edition. We may be quite certain, therefore, that unlike Dr. Percy Trevelyan's monograph on obscure nervous lesions, the book was not the subject of any discouraging reports from the publishers.[7] It is, however, sixteen years since it was published, and it is pertinent for us to wonder (and indeed to ask) why no further batches of Watson's unprinted records have been released.

It is true that in 1897 Holmes told Watson that "the world is not yet prepared" for the truth (presumably either defamatory or horrific) about the ship Matilda Briggs, which was "associated with the giant rat of Sumatra".[8] We must accept Holmes's word for it that the story was unpublishable over seventy years ago, but it may be thought that during the interim the world has had time to prepare itself suitably, and is indeed eager to know all about it. There was evidently a similar temporary embargo on one of the several "Second Stain" affairs in which Holmes became involved. Watson said in 1888 that the unpublished case to which this title was given "implicates so many of the first families in the kingdom, that for many years it will be impossible to make it public".[9] It may be thought that, as in the affair of the Matilda Briggs, the passage in this instance of

[1] *The Golden Pince-Nez*, S., p. 783.
[2] *The Hound of the Baskervilles*, L., p. 442.
[3] *Ibid.*, p. 321.  [4] *The Priory School*, S., p. 662.
[5] *Black Peter*, S., p. 697.  [6] *A Scandal in Bohemia*, S., p. 24.
[7] *The Resident Patient*, S., p. 460.  [8] *The Sussex Vampire*, S., p. 1178.
[9] *The Naval Treaty*, S., p. 498. The published case, of course, implicated only Lady Hilda Trelawney Hope, who was in Watson's opinion, "the most lovely woman in London", *The Second Stain*, S., p. 869.

over eighty years would have removed any difficulties. I am not aware of any insuperable problems of publication in other examples.

Obviously, the non-appearance of the eagerly awaited sequel (or sequels) to *The Exploits of Sherlock Holmes*, during so long a period as sixteen years, offers a mystery to be solved. I think that the most acceptable explanation is that during their researches, which would clearly be exhaustive, the authors discovered to their disappointment that only a fraction of Watson's literary remains had been preserved. They put this small amount of material to the utmost use, filling in the gaps with a good deal of most skilful literary improvisation. The result was a delight to Sherlockians, but inevitably there was nothing left over for any sequels.

I have found substantial support for this assumption in the text of the canon, and in *The Exploits of Sherlock Holmes*. In his single reference to one of the cases reconstructed in that book Watson wrote:

> "Somewhere in the vaults of the bank of Cox & Co., at Charing Cross, there is a travel-worn and battered tin dispatch box with my name, John H. Watson, M.D., Late Indian Army, painted upon the lid. It is crammed with papers, nearly all of which are records of cases to illustrate the curious problems which Mr. Sherlock Holmes had at various times to examine. Some, and not the least interesting, were complete failures, and as such will hardly bear narrating, since no final explanation is forthcoming. A problem without a solution may interest the student, but can hardly fail to annoy the casual reader. Among these unfinished tales is that of Mr. James Phillimore, who, stepping back into his own house to get his own umbrella, was never more seen in this world."[1]

It is clear from this that the notes on the disappearance of Mr. Phillimore in Watson's dispatch-box were an unfinished tale of one of Sherlock Holmes's "complete failures". Yet in the chapter "The Highgate Miracle" in *The Exploits of Sherlock Holmes* the mystery is solved and the whole matter cleared up.

[1] *Thor Bridge*, S., p. 1215. Watson mentioned two other "complete failures" or "unfinished tales" under the same reference. These were the cases of Isadora Persano and the cutter *Alicia*.

What the authors did is not too difficult to deduce. The case was of absorbing interest because of its apparent sheer impossibility on the face of it. They wanted to include it, and by a process of highly ingenious speculation they worked out what seemed to them the most probable solution. Being completely honest men, they gave the astute reader a strong hint that the story they told was not necessarily one of historical fact, by giving Mr. James Phillimore an alias (until the last page) and calling him Mr. James Cabpleasure.[1]

The authors also seem to have encountered a difficulty in regard to "the Arnsworth Castle business", which they recorded as "The Red Widow" in *The Exploits of Sherlock Holmes*. In the text of the canon, Holmes said to Watson:

> "When a woman thinks that her house is on fire, her instinct is at once to rush to the thing which she values most. It is a perfectly overpowering impulse, and I have more than once taken advantage of it. In the case of the Darlington Substitution Scandal it was of use to me, and also in the Arnsworth Castle business. A married woman grabs at her baby—an unmarried one reaches for her jewel box."[2]

It is true that in "The Red Widow" the mystery was solved by the expedient of Holmes starting a small fire of straw in the cloakroom at Arnsworth Castle. It was not, however, a woman who was deceived by this simple stratagem in the reconstruction of the affair in *The Exploits of Sherlock Holmes*. The authors found it necessary to change the sex of the "rusher-to-save-the-thing-she-values-most-when-she-thinks-the-house-is-on-fire". and it was the aged and loyal manservant Stephen who was shocked into betraying the hiding-place of Lord Cope:

> " 'Fire! The house is on fire!' he shrieked. 'Oh, my master! My Lord! My Lord!'
> Holmes's hand fell upon his shoulder. 'A bucket of water in the cloakroom will meet the case', he said quietly. 'It would be as well, however, if you would ask his Lordship to join us.'

[1] *The Exploits of Sherlock Holmes*, p. 110. One wonders if the unlikely name of Cabpleasure was inspired by a recollection of Holmes's playful twitting of Watson on the subject of the doctor's enjoyment of the company of a lady in his cab. (*Lady Frances Carfax*, S., pp. 1018–19.)

[2] *A Scandal in Bohemia*, S., p. 24.

The old man sprang at him, his eyes blazing and his fingers crooked like the talons of a vulture.

'A trick!' he screamed. 'I've betrayed him through your cursed tricks!' "[1]

I suggest that in this case Watson's full notes on the Arnsworth Castle mystery were not available, and that the authors, with great ingenuity, created a superstructure of speculation as to what might have occurred in that "great building, its walls and turrets stark and grey against the night sky".[2] It is not easy to understand in what other circumstances they would have found it necessary to depart from the central psychological point of Holmes's discourse to Watson.

There are other examples. I think, however, that the answer to all these questions is contained in the text of *The Exploits of Sherlock Holmes*, where it is stated that the material available to Mr. Adrian Conan Doyle and Mr. John Dickson Carr was limited to some "notebooks" of Watson's, preserved in a black "deed-box where they have been kept in recent years."[3] This was obviously not the large "dispatch-box", with "John H. Watson, M.D., Late Indian Army, painted on the lid", which we recall was "crammed with papers", without any mention of notebooks.[4] It was this immense mass of papers, as Watson said, that formed the main body of his notes, and contained the records of most of the unpublished cases to which he made reference in the canon. This circumstance would explain why the affair of Madame Taupin's wax-works, fully recorded under the title of "The Wax Gamblers" in *The Exploits of Sherlock Holmes*, was never mentioned by Watson. It was one of the lesser cases (perhaps not sufficiently concerned with Holmes's powers of observation and deduction) which had been consigned to the less important notebooks discovered in the deed-box.

If these assumptions are well-founded (and it is difficult to see how the facts can otherwise be explained) then we are entitled to wonder why the majority of Watson's notes have never been discovered. I fear that the most likely theory, a development of a view held by a great Holmesian scholar, the late Gavin Brend, must of necessity involve us in a scrutiny of

[1] *The Exploits of Sherlock Holmes*, p. 305.     [2] *Ibid.*, p. 295.
[3] *Ibid.*, p. 312.     [4] *Thor Bridge*, S., p. 1215.

some painful events in the later years of the life of Dr. Watson. Brend believed that the last Mrs. Watson, the bride of 1902, firmly opposed her husband's continuance as Holmes's biographer:

> "The visits to Holmes were very few. She did not demand a complete break with Holmes. To suggest that would be an exaggeration. But in her view such visits should be for social purposes only. Watson would be wasting his time if he accompanied Holmes on his adventures or wrote up his cases. Naturally this was just the sort of Mrs. Watson *not* to suit Sherlock Holmes. Hence his acid remark on Watson's selfishness in marrying her."[1]

Brend suggested that Watson first tried to defy his wife in regard to this cruel embargo, and then for a time continued to write up Holmes's cases in secret:

> "After Mrs. Watson had expressed her displeasure that he was still acting as Holmes's recorder, he came to the conclusion that disguise was essential. His first experiment was to write *The Mazarin Stone* in the third person. But . . . even if he were acquitted of the charge of authorship, he was still open to the accusation that he had wasted his time by accompanying Holmes on the case. So the deception was carried a further stage in *The Blanched Soldier*, which purports to be written by Holmes in Watson's absence."[2]

If Brend's belief approached the truth of the matter, it is not difficult to see that this fundamental matrimonial difference could well have ended in bitter quarrels. So far as Watson was concerned, his wife's criticisms would cut very deep. As he himself said, he had co-operated with Holmes, his best friend, and acted as his biographer for seventeen years.[3] He could not help but compare with nostalgia his fifth wife's interference and antagonism with the tolerance and understanding of that of his third matrimonial partner, Mary Watson. As Brend wrote:

> "[Mary] thought that her husband's true vocation was to act as Holmes's historian. Never mind his practice. Anstruther

---

[1] Brend, p. 172. "The good Watson had at that time deserted me for a wife, the only selfish action which I can recall in our association. I was alone." (*The Blanched Soldier*, S., p. 1118.)      [2] *Ibid.*, p. 174.
[3] *The Veiled Lodger*, S., p. 1287.

or Jackson or anyone else suitable could look after that.[1] The result was that the practice languished,[2] but Watson was given every possible encouragement by his wife to visit Holmes. He looked pale and needed a change[3] . . . The client was an old schoolfellow, so Watson must accompany him.[4] At any time of the day or night he would forsake everything, and with a hurried message to his wife would dash off to join Holmes.[5] His wife never complained."[6]

It is of great interest to notice in this connexion that Miss Dorothy Sayers had already suggested some years earlier that Watson's most unsuitable final marriage caused Holmes such unhappiness that this was the reason for his premature retirement from practice at the early age of fifty-one:

"Holmes, the man of iron, lost heart and set *finis* to his life's work. The autumn of life had breathed its chilling influence on both of them. So much for the 1902 marriage."[7]

The text of the canon makes it tragically clear that for some years after Holmes had retired to the South Downs in 1903, the fifth Mrs. Watson undoubtedly had her way. The two old friends were almost completely parted, and Holmes had to record his encounter with the deadly *Cyanea Capillata* himself:

"At this period of my life the good Watson had passed almost beyond my ken. An occasional week-end visit was the most that I ever saw of him. Thus I must act as my own chronicler. Ah! had he but been with me, how much he might have made of so wonderful a happening and of my eventual

---

[1] *The Boscombe Valley Mystery*, S., p. 75. "Oh, Anstruther would do your work for you." *The Crooked Man*, S., p. 441. "Could you go as far as Aldershot tomorrow?" "I have no doubt Jackson would take my practice."

[2] *The Red-Headed League*, S., p. 43. "I have nothing to do today. My practice is never very absorbing."

[3] *The Boscombe Valley Mystery*, S., p. 75. "You have been looking a little pale lately. I think that the change would do you good, and you are always so interested in Mr. Sherlock Holmes's cases."

[4] *The Naval Treaty*, S., p. 500. "My wife agreed with me that not a moment should be lost in laying the matter before [Holmes], and so, within an hour of breakfast-time, I found myself back once more in the old rooms in Baker Street.'

[5] *The Stockbroker's Clerk*, S., p. 356. " 'My client is outside in a four-wheeler. Can you come at once?' 'In an instant.' I scribbled a note to my neighbour, rushed upstairs to explain the matter to my wife, and joined Holmes upon the doorstep."

[6] Brend, pp. 171–2.

[7] *Unpopular Opinions*, p. 155.

triumph against every difficulty! As it is, however, I must needs tell my tale in my own plain way."[1]

These revealing sentences, surely the most melancholy in the whole saga, refrained significantly from any mention of the detested Mrs. Watson. The week-end visits were clearly by Watson alone, doubtless preceded and followed by bitter scenes with his wife. These acts of defiance and their accompanying penalties, however, were obviously so few and far between that they did not prevent Holmes observing, with infinite sadness, that Watson had virtually passed out of his old companion's life altogether.

The canon is entirely silent, as we might expect, about the fifth Mrs. Watson, apart from the bare record of the fact that Watson married her in 1902. Watson, an ex-officer and a gentleman, did not publicise his unhappiness. Miss Dorothy Sayers, with great penetration, provided a clue to both the situation and the lady concerned when she said that to Holmes the marriage probably "seemed merely wanton" on the part of Watson, who was fifty years old in 1902.[2] This confirms my own opinion that Watson, like many widowers of his difficult age, vainly seeking to perpetuate the illusions and pleasures of youth, married a woman of extreme sexual attraction many years younger than himself. Her selfish lack of any understanding of the bond between himself and Holmes, forged by their countless adventures together, would not become apparent until after the marriage. It is clear that for some years her physical charms continued to be irresistible to the infatuated Watson, for only in this way can we account for his going as far as he did to meet her cruelly intolerant objections to the continuance of his association with Holmes.

We know with thankfulness, however, that on 2 August, 1914, "the most terrible August in the history of the world"[3] Watson was reunited with Holmes, and in the latter's words, was "the same blithe boy as ever".[4] The chains of sensuality that had bound him ashamedly to the fifth Mrs. Watson had been finally broken forever, and with infinite pleasure he had joined his old friend as in days gone by, this time to assist in

---

[1] *The Lion's Mane*, S., pp. 1266–7.
[3] *His Last Bow*, S., p. 1068.

[2] *Unpopular Opinions*, p. 153.
[4] *Ibid.*, p. 1081.

the outwitting and capture of the German master spy Von Bork, "a man who could hardly be matched among all the devoted agents of the Kaiser".[1] It is a delight to quote the words in which Watson, with a lack of restraint unusual for him, expressed his relief that he was free at last and at his friend's side once more:

> "I feel twenty years younger, Holmes. I have seldom felt so happy as when I got your wire asking me to meet you at Harwich."[2]

We can deduce from the text of the canon, moreover, that this was the first meeting of the two friends for some years, so that it can confidently be inferred that Watson's separation from his wife was quite recent. The old campaigner's ordeal, which he would probably have conceded he had brought upon himself by the disastrous final indulgence in his life-long weakness for the opposite sex, had lasted twelve years:

> " 'But you, Watson,' [Holmes] stopped his work and took his old friend by the shoulders; 'I've hardly seen you in the light yet. How have the years used you. "[3]

All was well, despite the fact that England was on the brink of war with Germany. Holmes and Watson, though both now sixty-two, would naturally place their skill and experience at the disposal of their country, and Watson, indeed, was about to rejoin the Army Medical Service. Holmes anticipated, however, that in view of his age his friend would serve in an English military hospital, and that even during the exigencies of war there would still be occasional opportunities for them to spend an evening together in London, when we may be sure that the tantalus and the gasogene would be in evidence:

> "As to you, Watson, you are joining [up] with your old service, as I understand, so London won't be out of your way."[4]

This sounds as if Holmes had a comfortable *pied-à-terre* in London in 1914, presumably for his work for the Government, as well as his country house in Sussex. Dare we think that he had managed to secure the old rooms in Baker Street?

[1] *His Last Bow*, S., p. 1069.     [2] *Ibid.*, p. 1081.
[3] *Ibid.*, p. 1081.     [4] *Ibid.*, p. 1085.

Now that some aspects of the character of the fifth Mrs. Watson have been ascertained from an examination of the evidence, we may properly speculate upon her likely reactions to Watson leaving her during that fateful summer of 1914. The fact that her physical attractions (which had doubtless faded perceptibly during twelve years of marriage) were no longer capable of holding Watson, would certainly precipitate the hell and fury traditionally associated with women in her situation. We may assume with some confidence, moreover, that she would regard Holmes as mainly responsible for Watson's desertion of the marital home in Queen Anne Street. It follows that the inevitable short-term spleen-venting, in part at least, would be furiously directed at anything in the house connected with Watson's association with Holmes.

We already know that the large dispatch-box, "crammed with papers", had been removed from the vaults of the bank of Cox & Co. to Queen Anne Street soon after the marriage of 1902 to enable Watson secretly to write up, for example, the cases of *The Mazarin Stone* and *The Blanched Soldier*. We may assume that when Watson left Queen Anne Street for the last time he would take with him his notebooks, which were readily portable. One hesitates to suggest that Watson's departure would necessarily be accompanied by volleys of crockery flung in his wake by his infuriated wife, but we may at least be certain that the event would take place in circumstances of haste and urgency, and that the heavy dispatch-box would perforce be left behind. We can imagine the rest; the enraged forcing open of the lid with the kitchen poker and the vicious satisfaction of the lighting of the bonfire in the garden.

These are large assumptions, but it may be thought that they have a ring of authenticity about them. They offer a most plausible reason for the otherwise inexplicable omission by the authors of *The Exploits of Sherlock Holmes* to publish Watson's records of such obviously dramatic cases as those, for example, which were crowded into one vintage year alone:

"The year '87 furnished us with a long series of cases of greater or less interest, *of which I retain the records* [my italics]. Among my headings under this one twelve months, I find an account of the adventure of the Paradol Chamber, of the Amateur Mendicant Society, who held a luxurious club in the lower vault of a furniture warehouse, of the facts connected with the loss of the British barque *Sophy Anderson* [and] of the singular adventures of the Grice Patersons in the island of Uffa . . . All these I may sketch out at some future date."[1]

We thus have Watson's word for it that he had prepared notes on all these affairs, and it is surely reasonable to believe that if Mr. Adrian Conan Doyle and Mr. John Dickson Carr had discovered the relevant papers they would not have been so cruel as to fail to publish them. It is equally certain that if in Watson's notebooks they had found the explanation of the obviously unusual motives at work in the Dundas separation case, they could not have been so uncharitable as to keep it to themselves:

"The husband was a teetotaller, there was no other woman, and the conduct complained of was that he had drifted into the habit of winding up every meal by taking out his false teeth and hurling them at his wife."[2]

The deep interest of Sherlockians apart, the unique plight of Mrs. Dundas would clearly have provided invaluable research material for sociologists and Marriage Guidance Councils if the details had not been destroyed. Mrs. Watson had much for which to answer. Another example of a record of outstanding interest, which we know must have been amongst Watson's notes because of the terms in which Holmes referred to it, was almost certainly included in the bonfire at Queen Anne Street:

"You will remember, Watson, how the dreadful business of the Abernetty family was first brought to my notice by the depth which the parsley had sunk into the butter upon a hot day."[3]

In an earlier work I made some suggestions in regard to two cases mentioned without any details by Watson, mainly because I believed, as I still do, that he inserted them into the text for a deliberate and special purpose.[4] These were the affairs of "the whole story concerning the politician, the lighthouse and the

---

[1] *The Five Orange Pips*, S., p. 103.   [2] *A Case of Identity*, S., p. 56.
[3] *The Six Napoleons*, S., p. 743.   [4] Hall, pp. 107–8.

trained cormorant"[1] and "the singular tragedy of the Atkinson brothers at Trincomalee".[2] Lacking as I do, however, the imagination and the literary skill of Mr. Adrian Conan Doyle and Mr. John Dickson Carr, it is beyond my capability to compose any acceptable pastiches based on the unpublished cases myself. In the opposite circumstances, however, there is not the slightest doubt which one I would choose to attempt. Watson's reference to it is limited to a single sentence written in 1900:

> "A third case worthy of note is that of Isadora Persano, the well-known journalist and duellist, who was found stark staring mad with a matchbox in front of him which contained a remarkable worm, said to be unknown to science."[3]

What an array of problems this case offers for our attention! An amusing reconstruction of the case by Mr. Stuart Palmer was published in 1944.[4] According to him, Mr. Isadora Persano was a journalist and a Christian Scientist, whose controversial articles in *The Sketch* attacking the medical profession had justifiably aroused the extreme annoyance of the doctors. Persano had even been challenged to a duel by the Secretary of the Royal College of Surgeons. In the event this had turned out to be a very milk-and-water affair, honour apparently being satisfied by the two duellists firing harmlessly over each other's heads.

Still fearful over the enmity he had attracted to himself, however, Persano collapsed in Oxford Street and to his horror regained consciousness in Charing Cross Hospital, completely in the power of the doctors. The remarkable worm, whose "strange and repellent appearance" was presumably calculated to drive him to insanity when he set eyes on it, had been left in a bottle by his bedside to await his return to consciousness. Terrified, but still sane, he seized his clothes and the bottle and fled to Baker Street for protection and sanctuary.

Holmes thought that the worm was "a representative of the *phylla* group—possibly one of the *Platyhelminthes*, but most certainly of a venomous breed hitherto unknown to science".

---

[1] *The Veiled Lodger*, S., p. 1288.    [2] *A Scandal in Bohemia*, S., p. 4.
[3] *Thor Bridge*, S., p. 1215.
[4] "The Adventure of the Remarkable Worm." *The Misadventures of Sherlock Holmes*, (Boston, 1944), pp. 108–15.

He was, however, corrected by Watson, who confessed that this was a moment for which he had been waiting for many years, since 1881 in fact, "when Holmes talked me into giving away Fusilier, my bull pup, on the grounds that the poor fellow snored".[1] Watson explained that it was perfectly obvious to a medical man that Persano was seized with a sudden and severe intestinal attack while walking in Oxford Street. When he was removed to Charing Cross Hospital an emergency operation was found to be necessary. He was left to regain consciousness unattended, with the evidence of the operation in a bottle beside his bed. "Floating in a clear viscous liquid was an object both strange and repellent, a slender wormlike creature no more than six inches in length, with an eyeless, swollen head". As Watson remarked, this unpleasant object might be unknown to *Christian* science, but was nothing more than Persano's infected vermiform appendix.

This is an ingenious story, demolished, I fear, by its opening sentences describing the weather in Baker Street:

"Sherlock Holmes turned abruptly away from the bay window against which all day a raw April wind had been driving rain. The spring of '93 will be remembered as unusually inclement, even for London, and as always the dreariness of the weather conspired with professional inactivity to force Holmes farther and farther into the depths of black depression."

In 1893, of course, Holmes was still presumed to be dead, and was not to cause Watson to faint by his reappearance until 1894. Whether in April, 1893, Holmes was still in Khartoum or had arrived at Montpelier to spend "some months in a research into the coal-tar derivatives"[2] is not capable of precise calculation from the text of the canon, but he was certainly not in Baker Street. This apart, I fear that by his failure to comment upon the fact that Isadora is the name of a woman, Mr. Palmer has demonstrated his lack of comprehension of what the Persano case was about. It was an appalling business, and is worthy of our close examination.

[1] It will be recalled that when Watson agreed to share the Baker Street lodging with Holmes he referred to his bull-pup (*A Study in Scarlet*, L., p. 13) and that this animal is never mentioned again throughout the entire canon.

[2] *The Empty House*, S., p. 569.

As I tried to show in my earlier book, Watson was capable of occasional literary subtlety, as was demonstrated by his references to both the politician/lighthouse/cormorant affair and that of the Atkinson brothers at Trincomalee. In the macabre Persano case we have another example. Watson made no direct comment upon the obvious contradiction that Persano, described by Watson as "him", flaunted a woman's forename. In considering this lack of explanation of a very curious fact, it is relevant to recall the essential personality of Watson. He was "a middle-sized, strongly built man" with a square jaw, a thick neck and a military moustache.[1] He was an ex-officer and a former Rugby player.[2] In middle life his normal relaxations from the calls of duty as Holmes's biographer were playing billiards at his club,[3] reading Clark Russell's "fine sea stories"[4] and spending half his wound pension on racing.[5] He was devoted to the fair sex and was married five times. It would be hard to find a more typical example of the down-to-earth, heterosexual, extroverted Englishman, who (especially in the non-permissive society of the end of the nineteenth century) would recoil from discussion in print of sexual problems of any kind.

Watson was, however, a conscientious recorder of Holmes's cases. He was not prepared to say that Isadora Persano was a transvestite in so many words, but instead offered a definite clue to the serious researcher by his description of Persano as a well-known *duellist*. This was inherently improbable on the face of it, and I feel sure that Watson was telling us as clearly as he could, within the limits of the phonetic and semantic possibilities available to him, that Persano was a *dualist*. This was a most ingenious if not entirely accurate description of one of those men of two-fold nature who cannot resist at times an urge to dress themselves in women's clothes and exhibit other feminine characteristics. Persano's shameless use of the forename Isadora demonstrates beyond doubt that he was an extreme case of transvestism.

When a mystery presents two bizarre features it is extremely probable, on the theory of Occam's razor, that these oddities

---

[1] *Charles Augustus Milverton*, S., p. 738.  [2] *The Sussex Vampire*, S., p. 1182.
[3] *The Dancing Men*, S., p. 611.  [4] *The Five Orange Pips*, S., p. 104.
[5] *Shoscombe Old Place*, S., p. 1301.

will be connected. As a working hypothesis, therefore, we may assume that the "remarkable worm, said to be unknown to science" was sent to Persano to cause his stark staring madness *because of his activities as a transvestite.* We can, incidentally, be reasonably certain that the deadly worm was sent in its matchbox anonymously through the post. Its bite caused incurable insanity, and we may presume that Persano was bitten when he innocently opened the box. We can, I fancy, discount the possibility that the mere appearance of the creature was so horrific that this alone was sufficient to cause madness. It may well have been unpleasant-looking and quite unlike the "poor helpless worms" to which Holmes referred with sympathy during the tragic case of John Turner,[1] but its small size would surely prevent it being sufficiently frightening to drive Persano out of his mind.

Who sent the worm and why? Before we can answer this question we must examine the case of *The Three Gables*, in which (although it has never been suggested before) the transvestite Isadora played a leading role, this time as a woman calling "herself" Isadora Klein. The affair was concerned with the death of Douglas Maberley and the mysterious events that followed in his mother's house at Harrow Weald. Maberley died (actually of pneumonia but virtually of a broken heart) because the "woman" whom he passionately loved not only refused to marry him, but because of his importunities hired a gang of ruffians to beat him up and so drive him away. Before his death he wrote a novel, with thinly disguised identities, describing the brutal treatment he had received and the sufferings he had undergone. It seems probable that there were other revelations about the "lady" concerned. Isadora Klein said to Holmes:

> "He wrote to me and sent me a copy of his book that I might have the torture of anticipation. There were two copies, he said—one for me, one for his publisher . . . Then came Douglas's sudden death. So long as that other manuscript was in the world there was no safety for me. Of course, it must be among his effects, and these would be returned to his mother. I set the gang at work. One of them got into the

[1] *The Boscombe Valley Mystery*, S., p. 102.

house as a servant. I wanted to do the thing honestly. I really and truly did. I was ready to buy the house and everything in it. I offered any price [Mrs. Maberly] cared to ask. I only tried the other way when everything else had failed."[1]

The "other way", when the attempt at purchase of the house and its contents was rebuffed, was the burglary of *The Three Gables* and the stealing and destruction of the dangerously embarrassing manuscript, of which the last page was left behind by accident. The end of the affair was that Holmes decided that he would "have to compound a felony, as usual",[2] and extracted a cheque for £5,000 from Isadora as the price of his silence, to enable Douglas Maberley's mother to realise her ambition to travel round the world. There can be little doubt that the "lady" who paid over so large a sum as this (in the nineteenth century) to preserve the secrets of "her" sex life from publication was Isadora Persano, later to become entangled with the remarkable worm and be driven "stark staring mad".

H. W. Bell and Gavin Brend, two leading Sherlockian biographers, respectively placed *The Three Gables* as occurring in May and September, 1903.[3] This year is, however, much too late, and the evidence upon which the estimate was based is very vulnerable. It relied mainly on the fact that Watson was not living at Baker Street ("I had not seen Holmes for some days")[4] during the Maberley affair, and that the action therefore took place during one of his periods of marriage. Bell (who believed that Watson was married only three times) wrote:

"Watson has left Baker Street [to be married]. The possible years are (*a*) during his first marriage, i.e. 1888–90; (*b*) 1896; (*c*) 1902–3. It will be remembered that Douglas Maberley at the time of his death was in the diplomatic service; and his book, which was obviously autobiographical, was too scandalous to have been published by a man in his position during Queen Victoria's reign."[5]

The argument that the dates of 1888–90 and 1896 must be ruled out relied entirely upon the assertion that the book was

[1] *The Three Gables*, S., p. 1177.    [2] *Ibid.*, S., p. 1177.
[3] *Chronology*, p. 117 and Brend, p. 180.    [4] *The Three Gables*, S., p. 1159.
[5] *Chronology*, p. 117.

scandalous in its contents. This has no evidence to support it, for of course only the last sheet of the manuscript, p. 245, was preserved, containing four sentences and part of a sentence.[1] No book can be judged on so small a sample. For what it is worth, I may say that the comment by the local "bustling, rubicund Inspector"[2] that it "seemed mighty poor stuff"[3] echoes my own opinion of the literary quality of the only surviving page of the late Mr. Douglas Maberley's manuscript.

With all this out of the way, I can now say that I have not the slightest doubt that the case of *The Three Gables* and Isadora Klein took place during the first years of Watson's marriage to Mary Morstan, and that the affair of Isadora Persano occurred not long afterwards, certainly before October of 1889,[4] for which proof is available. In my first book I showed that as late as 1881 Holmes had definite leanings towards mysticism and other facets of occultism, exemplified by his remark to Watson that there were "vague memories in our souls of those misty centuries when the world was in its childhood".[5] The great detective's solution of the mystery of the death in 1888 of Edmund Gurney, the Hon. Secretary of the Society for Psychical Research, however, ultimately transformed Holmes's views on these matters to militant scepticism. Several apposite extracts from the canon were quoted to document my original argument in regard to Holmes's complete change of heart,[6] but a couple of references are sufficient for our present purpose.

"But are we to give serious attention to such things? This Agency stands flat-footed upon the ground, and there it must remain. The world is big enough for us. No ghosts need apply."[7]

This complete conversion had clearly taken place by October, 1889,[8] when (after yawning and tossing his cigarette-end into the fire) Holmes told Dr. James Mortimer that the latter's story

---

[1] *The Three Gables*, S., p. 1172.    [2] *Ibid.*, S., p. 1169.    [3] *Ibid.*, S., p. 1172.
[4] Bell, in company with all other biographers, regarded this case as undatable. (*Chronology*, p. 130).
[5] *A Study in Scarlet*, L., p. 46. The down-to-earth Watson's tactful comment, "That's rather a broad idea", was revealing.
[6] Hall, pp. 109–11.
[7] *The Sussex Vampire*, S., p. 1179.
[8] This incontrovertible dating of the Baskerville case is documented by Blakeney, p. 71.

of the curse of the Baskervilles, the "dreadful apparition, exactly corresponding to the hell-hound of the legend", could only be of interest "to a collector of fairy-tales".[1] Holmes's most significant remark of all in this context (because it placed him squarely in the opposite camp) was his remonstrance that Dr. Mortimer had "quite gone over to the supernaturalists".[2]

With the facts established, it is quite clear that by October, 1889 any leanings towards a magical view of the world by Holmes had been entirely dispelled. His concept of the universe was by this time entirely and almost aggressively scientific. The idea of a worm "said to be unknown to science" was therefore impossible by then so far as he was concerned. It inevitably follows that the Persano affair took place prior to October, 1889. If the Maberley case occurred some months earlier during the early months of Watson's marriage to Mary Morstan and his consequent absence from Baker Street, as demonstrated by the text of *The Three Gables*, then the factual chronology is settled.

There is no doubt about Mrs. Maberley's opinion of Isadora Klein, who had caused the death of her beloved son, for she expressed it to Holmes:

" 'You remember him as he was—debonair and splendid. You did not see the moody, morose, brooding creature into which he developed. His heart was broken. In a single month I seemed to see my gallant boy turn into a worn-out cynical man'.
'A love affair—a woman?'
'Or a fiend'."[3]

We shall probably never know whether Douglas Maberley ever discovered that Isadora Klein, "roguish and exquisite"[4] yet "masterful",[5] was the transvestite who some months later reverted, possibly publicly, to "her" masculine role of Isadora Persano. We can, however, imagine the emotions of Mrs. Maberley when the incredible facts came to her notice. We can be sure that they did, for she would naturally be interested in the subsequent career of the creature who had ruined her

---

[1] *The Hound of the Baskervilles*, L., p. 286.      [2] *Ibid.*, p. 295.
[3] *The Three Gables*, S., p. 1162.
[4] *Ibid.*, p. 1176. It is significant, perhaps, that in "her" feminine role, Isadora's face appeared "mask-like" (*Ibid.*, p. 1174) doubtless due to heavy make-up.
[5] *Ibid.*, p. 1173.

son and caused his tragic death. All thoughts of her proposed trip round the world would vanish; she would think only in terms of as terrible a vengeance as was possible.

In 1889 Professor Moriarty was very much alive and in business. Holmes said of him in 1891, we remember:

> "He sits motionless, like a spider in the centre of its web, but that web has a thousand radiations, and he knows well every quiver of each of them. He does little himself. He only plans. But his agents are numerous and splendidly organized. Is there a crime to be done, a paper to be abstracted, we will say, a house to be rifled, a man to be removed—the word is passed to the Professor, the matter is organized and carried out."[1]

It is curious that Holmes should have mentioned both the rifling of a house and the abstraction of papers as two examples of the kind of crime for which the Moriarty organization could be hired at a substantial fee, for to Holmes's knowledge this was precisely what had happened at *The Three Gables*. We know also that it was done by a "gang"[2] under the leadership of Barney Stockdale, but that Holmes sensed the existence of a sinister, higher intelligence behind the scenes:

> "What I want to know is, who is at the back of them on this particular occasion?"[3]

If, as now seems most probable, the Moriarty organization was employed by Isadora (Klein) Persano to obtain the Maberley manuscript, the Professor would be fully aware of all the facts and of the events that followed. He would know that due to Holmes's intervention Mrs. Maberley had become possessed of the considerable sum of £5,000 and was thirsting for revenge upon the person whom she most certainly regarded as the murderer of her son. The fact that the organization had previously acted for Persano would not weigh with Moriarty for a moment, we may think. Crime to him was simply a matter of business, in which there is no sentiment. The fee from Persano had been earned and that file was closed. What was now important was that Mrs. Maberley was a potential new client, with

[1] *The Final Problem*, S., p. 540.　　　[2] *The Three Gables*, S., p. 1169.
[3] *Ibid.*, p. 1161.

an unexpected £5,000 at her disposal, filled with seething fury at the discovery that her son's ruin and death had been brought about by a creature who was not a woman at all.

I am without information in regard to any code of professional conduct followed by master-criminals, and I do not know, therefore, whether the soliciting of instructions is prohibited or not. In the latter alternative, which seems the most probable, it may be thought that Mrs. Maberley was tactfully approached by one of Moriarty's agents, who were "numerous and splendidly organized". In this event, we can be certain that the assurance that efficient arrangements could be made for a sticky fate to overtake Persano, on the basis of £2,500 down and an equivalent amount on completion, would fall on willing ears.

Moriarty was a scientific person and was, in Holmes's words, "a genius, a philosopher, an abstract thinker" with "a brain of the first order". He was "the Napoleon of crime".[1] To the student of criminology it may seem that there is more than one suggestive parallel between the career of Professor Moriarty, who flourished in the latter part of the nineteenth century, and that of Dr. Fu-Manchu, who was at the height of his powers in the nineteen-twenties. After the death of Moriarty, Fu-Manchu succeeded him as "the most malign and formidable personality existing in the world today . . . an adept in all the arts and sciences which a great university could teach him . . . a mental giant."[2] It is, for example, a remarkable coincidence that the crimes of Fu-Manchu, like those of Moriarty, were recorded by a London physician who was the best friend of the investigator.[3]

The two master-criminals were clearly much alike in their intellectual powers and scientific resources, and it may be thought not improbable that Fu-Manchu studied his predecessor's methods and made use of some of them. This is admittedly speculative, but it can be said with certainty that for certain crimes Fu-Manchu employed deadly weapons not dissimilar in general terms from the remarkable worm used by Moriarty on Isadora Persano. The death of Sir Crichton Davey, for

---

[1] *The Final Problem*, S., p. 540.

[2] Sax Rohmer, *The Book of Fu-Manchu* (London, 1929), p. 26.

[3] Respectively Dr. Petrie and Nayland Smith. It must be conceded that when Smith, like Holmes, was offered a knighthood (*The Three Garridebs*, S., p. 1196) he failed to follow Holmes's modest example, and accepted it.

example, was caused by an unpleasant creature sent by Fu-Manchu:

> "It was an insect, full six inches long, and of a vivid, venomous red colour! It had something of the appearance of a great ant, with its long quivering antennae and its febrile, horrible vitality."[1]

It is of additional coincidental interest that murders of this kind arranged by Fu-Manchu were interspersed, by way of variety, by simply causing the victims to become insane. It may be thought that there is a striking similarity between the stark, staring madness of Persano as a result of the attentions of Moriarty's remarkable worm, and the condition of Inspector Weymouth following his exposure to Dr. Fu-Manchu's variety of the giant *empusa*. He became "a man who shrieked and fought like a savage animal, foamed at the mouth and gnashed his teeth in horrid frenzy . . . a madman".[2]

The fact that Fu-Manchu's deadly armoury included "centipedes whose poisonous touch, called 'the zayat kiss', is certain death; several species of scorpion . . . and some kind of bloated unwieldy spider, so gross of body that its short, hairy legs could scarce support it",[3] does not decrease the similarity between the two cases, for there is evidence in the canon that Moriarty's remarkable worm had a minimum of one bedfellow. Who can doubt, for example, the identity of the organisation and its scientific resources responsible for at least one horrific case of murder which Watson never published? Because of the bonfire in the back garden of Queen Anne Street our knowledge of the affair is limited to a single sentence by Watson, but it may be thought that this is sufficient to show that Moriarty had at least one other worm in his armoury of unusual weapons, this time a blood-sucker:

> "As I turn over the pages I see my notes upon the repulsive story of the red leech and the terrible death of Crosby the banker."[4]

I must concede that it is a monstrous impertinence on my part to attempt a reconstruction of the Persano affair. Watson

---

[1] *The Book of Fu-Manchu*, op. cit., p. 33.     [2] *Ibid.*, p. 241.
[3] *Ibid.*, p. 697.     [4] *The Golden Pince-Nez*, S., p. 783.

grouped it with the mysteries of Mr. James Phillimore and his umbrella, and "the cutter *Alicia*, which sailed one morning into a small patch of mist from which she never again emerged" as being among Holmes's "complete failures" and "unfathomed cases".[1] Despite the apparent perplexity of the Master, however, Mr. Stuart Palmer, Mr. John Dickson Carr and the late Mr. Adrian Conan Doyle have attempted to solve two of these three complex problems, as we have seen. My defence must be, therefore, that I am in respectable company.

[1] *Thor Bridge*, S., p. 1215.

# VII

## THE LATE MR. SHERLOCK HOLMES

Vincent Starrett, probably the leading authority in America on the literature of Baker Street,[1] wrote in 1934:

"But there can be no grave for Sherlock Holmes or Watson . . . Shall they not always live in Baker Street? . . . Are they not there this instant, as one writes? . . . Outside, the hansoms rattle through the rain, and Moriarty plans his latest devilry. Within, the sea-coal flames upon the hearth, and Holmes and Watson take their well-won ease . . . So they still live for all that love them well: in a romantic chamber of the heart: in a nostalgic country of the mind: where it is always 1895."[2]

When *The Private Life of Sherlock Holmes* was re-published in London in 1961, this passage in regard to the immortality of Holmes and Watson was repeated on p. 62.

Starrett's words are noble, and the sentiment they express must have an everlasting appeal for all Sherlockians. On the other hand, they are at variance with the text of the canon ( which to the fundamentalist must always be the final authority) on three chronological points. We know from Holmes himself that in 1902 Watson had married yet again and had left Baker Street forever,[3] whilst from the same first-hand source we must accept the fact that after 1903 Holmes himself had retired to the Sussex Downs, where Watson was merely an occasional week-

---

[1] An opinion expressed by Ellery Queen in *The Misadventures of Sherlock Holmes*, op. cit., p. 48, in his introduction to Starrett's pastiche, "The Unique Hamlet".
[2] Starrett, p. 87.     [3] *The Blanched Soldier*, S., p. 1118.

end visitor.[1] It may, of course, be urged that from Starrett's point of view a timeless 1895 was to be superimposed upon the years 1934 and 1961 when the passage was written, that the events described in the canon after 1895 were to be ignored, and that Holmes and Watson were therefore still living in Baker Street. To the sentimentalist such an illusion has an irresistible appeal, both to his imagination and to his sense of the past, but it does not overcome the third inevitable objection of the fundamentalist. In 1891, once more on the authority of Holmes as an eye-witness, Professor Moriarty had met a violent death at the Reichenbach:

"I slipped through his grip, and he with a horrible scream kicked madly for a few seconds and clawed the air with both his hands. But for all his efforts he could not get his balance, and over he went. With my face over the brink I saw him fall for a long way. Then he struck a rock, bounded off, and splashed into the water."[2]

It follows that there is no canonical authority for the continued planning of devilry by Moriarty in 1895.

I am by no means the first commentator to challenge the immortality of Holmes. E. E. Kellett's "Monody on the Death of Sherlock Holmes" was included in an admirable collection of Holmesian pieces edited by Edgar W. Smith and published in 1944.[3] More importantly, in recent years at least two attempts have been made to reconstruct Holmes's last days and the circumstances of his death. They differ widely in their conclusions, so that some critical scrutiny of them is perhaps both excusable and appropriate.

The late W. S. Baring-Gould asserted in 1962 that Sherlock Holmes died of old age on Sunday, 6 January, 1957.[4] The world's greatest detective had taken a solitary walk along the cliff path near his country villa on the evening of his 103rd birthday, a walk that had been one of the pleasures of his retirement "to my little Sussex home, when I had given myself up entirely to that soothing life of Nature for which I had so

---

[1] *The Lion's Mane*, S., p. 1266.  [2] *The Empty House*, S., p. 566.
[3] *Profile by Gaslight. An Irregular Reader about the Private Life of Sherlock Holmes* (New York, 1944), p. 137.
[4] Baring-Gould, pp. 245–9.

often yearned during the long years spent amid the gloom of London".[1] Holmes had described the scene himself, shortly after he had settled in his native county fifty-four years earlier:

"My villa is situated upon the southern slope of the Downs, commanding a great view of the Channel . . . On the morning of which I speak the wind had abated, and all Nature was newly washed and fresh. It was impossible to work upon so delightful a day, and I strolled out before breakfast to enjoy the exquisite air. I walked along the cliff path which led to the steep descent to the beach."[2]

According to Baring-Gould the old detective's carriage was erect and his snow-white hair was still thick, despite his 103 years. His "keen grey eyes were undimmed by the passing of the years". This miraculous defiance of extreme old age had been made possible by Holmes's remarkable discovery as a beekeeper that "royal jelly", produced by the pharyngeal glands of bees and fed in concentrated form to the larvae destined to become queens, could also preserve and prolong the process of human life. Holmes had shared this secret only with his brother Mycroft, to change the latter's "lethargy into dynamic energy" and to enable him (according to Baring-Gould) to serve Great Britain "through two world wars" as head of the British Secret Service. The "royal jelly" had so rejuvenated Mycroft that at the age of ninety-six he had scrambled energetically with the late Sir Winston Churchill from a landing-craft on to the North African shore.

Since these conjectures would of necessity involve us in the presumption that the effect of the "royal jelly" on the human body had been discovered by Holmes as early as World War I, it seems remarkable that he had not made it available to Watson, and so enabled his comrade of so many years also to become a centenarian. This mystery is not diminished by Baring-Gould's assertion that Watson's death "had been one of the greatest blows" Holmes had ever borne. According to Baring-Gould's story, Watson, that "firm friend, trusted companion [and] British gentleman" had died in 1929, only two years after the publication of *The Case-Book of Sherlock Holmes*, the final collection of Watson's accounts of Holmes's investigations, and three

[1] *The Lion's Mane*, S., p. 1266.    [2] *Ibid.*, pp. 1267–8.

years before he had reached the comparatively youthful age of eighty.

It is equally curious that Holmes's withholding of the secret of the apiarian elixir from everyone but Mycroft necessarily excluded his own son, who according to Baring-Gould was born to Irene Adler in 1892[1] and was therefore in his mid-sixties in 1957. By the age standards of Holmes and Mycroft those were, of course, almost formative years, but a devoted father, it may be thought, might nevertheless have considered the beneficial long-term effects that the boy would have enjoyed from an occasional dose of the "royal jelly".

Holmes's death was very peaceful. He stopped to rest on a bench beside the cliff path and "gazed far out across the rolling Channel, its customary grey reddened by the sinking sun". Holmes was content. His great work, *The Whole Art of Detection*, was finished at last:

> "Carefully wrapped, precisely addressed in his clear, copperplate handwriting, it lay on his study table. In the morning it would go to his publisher . . . How fitting that it should have been completed on this, his birthday. His one-hundred-and-third birthday!"[2]

According to Baring-Gould, in his final hour of life, serene and courageous to the end, the old detective recalled the days of the past and the personalities who had been inextricably bound up with the achievements of his long career. He thought, perhaps not too unkindly, of some of his former enemies, Dr. Grimesby Roylott, John Clay, John Stapleton (*alias* Baskerville), Colonel Sebastian Moran, Culverton Smith, Charles Augustus Milverton and above all, Professor James Moriarty, the Napoleon of crime. He remembered with pleasure his old rivals, Inspectors Gregson, Lestrade, MacDonald and Hopkins. His fondest memories were those of his brother and of his best friend, John Hamish Watson, but never once, if we accept Baring-Gould's story, did Holmes think of his son. His last thought was of his mistress, the boy's mother:

> "It had grown much colder, and very dark. The old man on the bench drew his caped overcoat still closer about him.

[1] Baring-Gould, p. 178.  [2] Baring-Gould, p. 245.

The grey eyes closed. The white-maned head fell forward on his breast. For the last time, the thin lips spoke. 'Irene', the old man said. 'Irene.'

Anderson of the Sussex Constabulary found him there in the morning."[1]

It is a pity that so moving and romantic a story as this, by so devoted a Sherlockian as the late W. S. Baring-Gould, should stimulate the kind of critical scrutiny at which I have hinted in my discussion of it. We cannot avoid, moreover, the recollection that in the same book he recklessly declared that Holmes was the third son of Siger and Violet Holmes and was born at their farmstead in the North Riding of Yorkshire,[2] an assertion at which I have previously ventured to raise a questioning eyebrow.[3] To an earnest Yorkshire student of the canon like myself such an idea is, of course, attractive in the extreme, and it is therefore all the more disappointing to have to draw attention to the incontrovertible evidence against it. What Yorkshireman, for example, would ever refer to Derbyshire, a county which is the very essence of the Midlands, as "the North of England" (as Holmes did),[4] or worse still, would say of his second visit to Donnithorpe in Norfolk, "of course I dropped everything and set out for the north once more"?[5]

We may fairly take into consideration, moreover, that another distinguished commentator, E. V. Knox, recorded that Holmes died in 1948:

"The death is announced at North Friston, near Eastbourne, of Mr. Sherlock Holmes, the eminent criminologist and investigator, President of the South Sussex Apiarist Society, and Corresponding Secretary to the National Beekeepers' Union. He was in his ninety-third year; and there is little doubt that but for his characteristic disregard of the occupational risks of this last hobby he would have lived to become a centenarian . . . His white hair and only slightly stooping figure had long been objects of veneration both to the passing motorist and to all residents of the countryside between Birling Gap and Newhaven."[6]

[1] Baring-Gould, p. 249.    [2] *Ibid.*, p. 11.    [3] Hall, pp. 18 and 38.
[4] *The Priory School*, S., p. 663.    [5] *The "Gloria Scott"*, S., p. 380.
[6] "The Passing of Sherlock Holmes", pp. 82–9, *Seventeen Steps to 221B. A Collection of Sherlockian Pieces by English Writers. With an Introduction by James*

A surprisingly contradictory detail was that Knox had not only nothing to tell us about Holmes's discovery of the miraculous life-giving properties of the "royal jelly", but actually asserted that the old detective was stung by one of his own bees, "possibly an Italian queen", and that this "was the immediate occasion of his demise".

Knox recorded, too, that Watson, far from dying in 1929, was elevated to the peerage and lived on until 1947. He said that Holmes's "old friend and colleague, the late Lord Watson of Staines . . . it will be remembered, died suddenly last year, after a particularly violent attack in the House of Lords upon certain provisions of the National Health Bill". These widely differing accounts by historians of events of such importance can be exceedingly confusing to the student, and I feel sure that my own doubts about both these two agreeable stories were shared by Sir Paul Gore-Booth (now Lord Gore-Booth, President of the Sherlock Holmes Society of London)[1] when he delivered an address on the life of Sherlock Holmes at St. Stephen's College, Delhi, on 8 August, 1961. He said:

"In 1903 Holmes seems to have retired from full-time detection and to have settled on the downs of Sussex to keep bees. From his retirement he completed one case and then, at the request of His Majesty's Government, made a dramatic re-appearance on the eve of World War I to expose an important German spy network. He retired again to Sussex. Nothing has been heard of him since, but it is of interest that there has been no death notice. It must therefore be assumed that at the age of 108, he is still alive and continues a placid life which, one hopes, was not too rudely interrupted by the events of 1940."[2]

It seems possible that Lord Gore-Booth, in believing that nothing had been heard of Holmes since 1914, had been misled by Sir Sydney Roberts:

*Edward Holroyd* (London, 1967). The essay was first published in *The Strand Magazine* in 1948.

[1] Sherlockians everywhere will share my hope that this belated but welcome recognition of the importance of the Presidency of the Society by the elevation of Sir Paul to the peerage will be automatic in the future. The appointment of Chief Valuer, Inland Revenue (to quote an example from my own profession) always carries a knighthood.

[2] *The Sherlock Holmes Journal*, Winter, 1961, p. 71.

"Of Holmes's way of life after 1914 no record survives. Whether he was ever again induced to leave his downland retreat seems doubtful."[1]

Sir Sydney's first sentence was, of course, at variance with the facts, which we may now appropriately examine. The penultimate collection of Holmes's case assembled by his devoted biographer, *His Last Bow*, was first published in October, 1917. Most fortunately for the historian and researcher, Watson contributed a short Preface:

"The friends of Mr. Sherlock Holmes will be glad to learn that he is still alive and well, though somewhat crippled by occasional attacks of rheumatism. He has, for many years, lived in a small farm upon the Downs five miles from Eastbourne, where his time is divided between philosophy and agriculture. During this period of rest he has refused the most princely offers to take up various cases, having determined that his retirement was a permanent one. The approach of the German war caused him, however, to lay his remarkable combination of intellectual and practical activity at the disposal of the Government, with historical results which are recounted in *His Last Bow*. Several previous experiences which have lain long in my portfolio, have been added to *His Last Bow* so as to complete the volume.

John H. Watson, M.D."

By contrast, when *The Case-Book of Sherlock Holmes* was published in 1927, Watson was ominously silent. A reassuring Preface to say that Holmes was "still alive and well" was conspicuous by its absence. It is difficult not to attach a sad significance to this complete omission, bearing in mind that ten years earlier Watson had clearly thought it both appropriate and important to publish a cheerful bulletin about his old comrade to "the friends of Mr. Sherlock Holmes". *The Case-Book* was, of course, merely a collection of Holmes's investigations all of which had occurred before his retirement in 1903, and its publication had no bearing upon the question as to whether he was still alive in 1927. The fact of the matter is that there is no evidence for Holmes's continued existence after October, 1917, when he was 65.[2]

[1] Roberts, pp. 16–17.
[2] Holmes was born in 1852. See Blakeney, p. 3 and Hall, p. 77.

I must say now that I have always thought it probable that Holmes died towards the end of World War I, and I believe, moreover, that there is some evidence to show either that in some curious way in 1914 he foresaw his own death from accident or natural causes, or that for a compelling reason he had by then decided to end his own life during the next few years. Looking at the first and least likely of these alternatives, it will be recalled that in my earlier book I tried to demonstrate that whilst in his later years Holmes's attitude towards spiritualism, extra-sensory perception and all the other paraphernalia of modern occultism was undoubtedly that of a militant sceptic, he had a contrasting trace of mysticism in his character which in early years occasionally showed itself. His famous dictum, "The world is big enough for us. No ghosts need apply"[1], is as well-known as his admiration for the writings of the rationalist William Winwood Reade.[2] On the other hand, his curious remark to Watson about music and soul-memories was clearly surprising to his biographer,[3] and perhaps might be accepted by some as not unconnected with his very occasional flashes of extraordinary intuition. I said in my previous book:

> "One wonders whether in the early 1880's, when Holmes still retained some of his leanings towards mysticism, there was any significance in a remark he made to Mr. Alexander Holder:
>
> > 'You owe a very humble apology to that noble lad, your son, who has carried himself in this matter as I should be proud to see my own son do, should I ever chance to have one.'[4]
>
> Taken in conjunction with Holmes's comment to Watson that he would never marry,[5] quoted earlier in this essay, this might be thought to be a rudimentary precognition of the future birth of his son out of wedlock."[6]

It may seem to some that Holmes's position in these matters was not dissimilar to that attributed to the late Harry Price

---

[1] *The Sussex Vampire*, S., p. 1179 and Hall, p. 110.
[2] *The Sign of Four*, L., p. 157 and Hall, pp. 109–10.
[3] *A Study in Scarlet*, L., pp. 45–6 and Hall, pp. 100–1.
[4] *The Beryl Coronet*, S., p. 269.          [5] *The Sign of Four*, L., p. 270.
[6] Hall, pp. 145–6.

in regard to the possibility of communication with the dead. "Scientifically, no; occasionally and spontaneously, yes."[1] Be that as it may, there can be no doubt that against the background of the absence of any evidence of Holmes being alive after 1917, two remarks of his to Watson in 1914 must be considered curious by any standards.

It was the late evening of the second day of August, 1914, "the most terrible August in the history of the world". Holmes and Watson, reunited after their long separation following Holmes's retirement and Watson's disastrous fifth marriage, were standing on the terrace of Von Bork's house on the cliffs near Harwich. The German master-spy had been ignominiously defeated, and the two old friends, now men of sixty-two, were together once more. It should have been a time for rejoicing, despite the imminence of war. Both Holmes and Watson would naturally serve their country to the utmost of their ability, but in view of their age neither would face the dangers of active service. They had every reason to suppose that the friendship that had been such a source of pleasure to both of them, now renewed, would survive the war. Yet Holmes said sombrely to his old companion:

"Stand with me here upon the terrace, for it may be the last quiet talk we shall ever have."[2]

A few moments later he added:

"There's an east wind coming all the same, such a wind as never blew on England yet. It will be cold and bitter, Watson, and a good many of us may wither before its blast."[3]

If Holmes did die during the war, as I shall suggest on the basis of other and possibly more factual considerations, then some may think that these sentences contain a suggestion of pre-cognition.

I am fully aware that my own theory that in 1914 Holmes had decided to end his own life in the not too distant future will be a grievous shock to all Holmesian scholars everywhere. Able minds and pens all over the world will energetically seek

---

[1] Paul Tabori, *Harry Price. The Biography of a Ghost Hunter.* (London, 1950), p. 3.
[2] *His Last Bow*, S., p. 1085.  [3] *Ibid.*, p. 1086.

to refute it, understandably and not unworthily, for subjective and sentimental reasons. An immediate objection, I think, will be that it is most unlikely that a man could calmly decide that life would become insupportable to him at some time in the future, and that when this final circumstance arose, and not before, he would commit suicide. I concede that such a time-lag in intention seems odd, but Holmes himself is my authority for saying that oddity in the circumstances of a mystery is an ingredient that usually assists in its solution:

" 'As a rule', said Holmes, 'the more bizarre a thing is the less mysterious it proves to be.' "[1]

"It is a mistake to confound strangeness with mystery . . . These strange details, far from making the case more difficult, have really had the effect of making it less so."[2]

Holmes made two other observations which would seem to support the series of inferences that I think can properly be drawn from the established fact of his addiction to tobacco.

" 'The ideal reasoner', he remarked, 'would, when he has once been shown a single fact in all its bearings, deduce from it not only the chain of events which led up to it, *but also all the results that would follow from it.* [my italics]. As Cuvier could correctly describe a whole animal by the contemplation of a single bone, so the observer who has thoroughly understood one link in a series of incidents, should be able accurately to state all the other ones, both before and after."[3]

This can be compared with Holmes's published remark in 1881 in *The Book of Life*:

"From a drop of water, a logician could infer the possibility of an Atlantic or a Niagara without having seen or heard of one or the other. So all life is a great chain, the nature of which is known whenever we are shown a single link of it."[4]

Holmes added an obvious qualification to these observations:

"To carry the art, however, to its highest pitch, it is necessary that the reasoner should be able to utilize all the facts which have come to his knowledge, and this in itself

[1] *The Red-Headed League*, S., pp. 42–3.     [2] *A Study in Scarlet*, L., p. 69.
[3] *The Five Orange Pips*, S., pp. 115–16.     [4] *A Study in Scarlet*, L., p. 20.

implies, as you will readily see, a possession of all knowledge, which, even in these days of free education and encyclopaedias, is a somewhat rare accomplishment."[1]

Tobacco amblyopia, as it is usually called, is an uncommon disease involving a slow build up of nicotine poisoning in the system through excessive smoking over a long period of years. Shag tobacco is especially harmful, and indulgence in alcohol stimulates the progress of the condition, which in time begins gradually to affect the eyesight. If the disease is diagnosed early enough, total and permanent abstinence from pipe-smoking especially will allow the system to clear itself from the poison over a period. There is, however, a point of no return in the development of the condition. If this is exceeded, nothing can be done and the eventual and inevitable result is total blindness.[2]

Holmes, of course, "smoked incessantly".[3] In company with the gasogene and the tantalus, a stock of cigars was permanently accessible in the Baker Street sitting-room, in a position affectionately described by Holmes to Watson as "the old place",[4] but which we know from Watson was the coal-scuttle.[5] We may notice, moreover, that Holmes clearly carried about with him a supplementary supply of cigars, from which he was able to offer one to Watson after lunch at Ross-on-Wye,[6] a hypothesis confirmed by the fact that in the Irene Adler affair Holmes "threw across his case of cigars" to Watson.[7] In parenthesis, it is worth mentioning that this latter case was wreathed in smoke of various kinds, of which Holmes must have breathed a great deal during its progress. He successfully combined the activities of "lighting a cigarette, and throwing himself down into an arm-chair".[8] After later deducing that the King of Bohemia's letter was written on paper made in Egria, he "sent up a great blue triumphant cloud from his cigarette".[9] Later

---

[1] *The Five Orange Pips*, S., p. 116.

[2] This discourse should not be taken as an impressive demonstration by me of the "possession of all knowledge" by an "ideal reasoner". The information came to me by chance. A friend of mine, a heavy pipe-smoker for thirty-five years, contracted tobacco amblyopia. He was fortunate in having his condition diagnosed in time.

[3] *The Second Stain*, S., p. 872.

[4] *The Mazarin Stone*, S., p. 1143.   [5] *The Musgrave Ritual*, S., p. 396.

[6] *The Boscombe Valley Mystery*, S., p. 95.   [7] *A Scandal in Bohemia*, S., p. 5.

[8] *Ibid.*, p. 6.   [9] *Ibid.*, p. 7.

still in the case, whilst disguised as "a drunken-looking groom, ill-kempt and side-whiskered",[1] Holmes smoked "two fills of shag tobacco" with the ostlers in the Serpentine Mews.[2] It speaks well for his versatility, moreover, to record that in order to bring the case to a successful conclusion, this time disguised as "an amiable and simple-minded Nonconformist clergyman", he cannot have failed to inhale a considerable quantity of the "thick clouds of smoke" pouring from the plumber's rocket which Watson had tossed into Irene Adler's sitting-room at Briony Lodge.[3]

There is abundant evidence to show that Holmes was an habitual cigarette smoker. Two examples of his addiction have been quoted, and there are many such single incidents throughout the canon. Whilst we may notice in passing that after yawning cavernously at Dr. Mortimer's "singular narrative" of the spectral hound, Holmes "tossed the end of his cigarette into the fire",[4] it is of greater significance to recall that after three days of absolute fasting his first need was for "a match and a cigarette."[5] It is of interest in this connexion to know that Holmes undoubtedly inhaled, for we are informed by Watson that the detective "drew in the smoke of his cigarette as if the soothing influence was grateful to him".[6] The text of the canon shows, moreover, that Holmes's consumption of cigarettes was large. On one occasion he told Watson that he had "a caseful of cigarettes here which need smoking",[7] and we recall that Professor Coram, who managed to get through seventy cigarettes a day, conceded that Holmes was a quicker smoker than himself.[8] This high compliment resulted from his watching the detective "consuming cigarette after cigarette' whilst lost in thought, lighting each "from the stub of that which he had finished".[9] In the McFarlane affair, after a night of concentrated thought (that left Holmes "pale and harassed") "the carpet round his chair was littered with cigarette ends".[10]

Despite the evidence for Holmes's liking for cigars and

[1] *A Scandal in Bohemia*, S., p. 14.     [2] *Ibid.*, p. 15.     [3] *Ibid.*, p. 23.
[4] *The Hound of the Baskervilles*, L., p. 286.
[5] *The Dying Detective*, S., p. 1015.
[6] *The Final Problem*, S., p. 538.
[7] *The Boscombe Valley Mystery*, S., p. 85.
[8] *The Golden Pince-Nez*, S., p. 798.     [9] *Ibid.*, pp. 798 and 799.
[10] *The Norwood Builder*, S., p. 600.

I

cigarettes, however, there can be no doubt regarding his even greater addiction to pipe tobacco. He measured the intricacy of the case of Mr. Jabez Wilson by calling it "quite a three-pipe problem", and forbade Watson to speak for fifty minutes as Holmes "sat with his eyes closed and his black clay pipe thrusting out like the bill of some strange bird".[1] This was, of course, "the old and oily clay pipe, which was to him as a counsellor",[2] in which he seems mainly to have smoked the strong shag which is claimed to be especially conducive to tobacco amblyopia:

> " 'When you pass Bradley's would you ask him to send up a pound of the strongest shag tobacco? Thank you. It would be as well if you could make it convenient not to return before evening.' . . . It was nearly nine o'clock when I found myself in the sitting-room once more. My first impression as I opened the door was that a fire had broken out, for the room was so filled with smoke that the light of the lamp upon the table was blurred by it. As I entered, however, my fears were set at rest, for it was the acrid fumes of strong, coarse tobacco, which took me by the throat and set me coughing. Through the haze I had a vague vision of Holmes in his dressing-gown coiled up in an arm chair with his black clay pipe between his lips. Several rolls of paper lay around him.
> 'Caught cold, Watson?' said he.
> 'No, it's this poisonous atmosphere.'
> 'I suppose it *is* pretty thick, now that you mention it.'
> 'Thick! It is intolerable.' "[3]

Shag was unquestionably Holmes's staple smoke, for when Watson modestly described himself as "an institution", it was to "the violin, the shag tobacco, the old black pipe [and] the index books" that he likened himself.[4] We recall that Holmes told Inspector Bradstreet that he solved the Neville St. Clair mystery "by sitting upon five pillows and consuming an ounce of shag",[5] and we can have little doubt of the source of the "slow wreaths of acrid tobacco [smoke]" that poured from his pipe during the Amberley case.[6]

[1] *The Red-Headed League*, S., p. 43.    [2] *A Case of Identity*, S., p. 65.
[3] *The Hound of the Baskervilles*, L., pp. 298.
[4] *The Creeping Man*, S., p. 1244.
[5] *The Man with the Twisted Lip*, S., p. 150.
[6] *The Retired Colourman*, S., p. 1321.

There can, of course, be no question about the huge quantity of shag consumed by Holmes. During the Baskerville affair he smoked continuously "all afternoon and late into the evening",[1] whilst earlier in the same case Holmes told Watson that during the latter's absence at his club he had drunk and smoked "two large pots of coffee and an incredible amount of tobacco".[2] At Poldhu Cottage Holmes smoked so hard and so long that "his haggard and ascetic face" became almost invisible to Watson "amid the blue swirl of his tobacco smoke",[3] just as the room became "full of a dense tobacco haze" when Holmes smoked all through the night at The Cedars at Lee, so that next morning "nothing remained of the heap of shag" which had been entirely consumed during this vigil.[4] Watson recorded that "for a whole day [before setting off for King's Pyland] my companion had rambled about the room with his chin upon his chest and his brows knitted, charging and re-charging his pipe with the strongest black tobacco."[5]

Another matter about which we can be certain is that Watson was acutely disturbed, with good reason, about his friend's excessive smoking. Holmes told Watson that he was "only a general practitioner with very limited experience",[6] but the evidence suggests that the anxious doctor was aware of the dangers of tobacco amblyopia and of the extreme likelihood of the disaster that faced Holmes in the years to come should he be prone to the disease. Watson warned his friend that he was "a self-poisoner by cocaine and tobacco",[7] whilst Holmes himself referred to "that course of tobacco-poisoning which you have so often and so justly condemned".[8] It may be thought that these sentences were significant and tragically prophetic, for we know, of course, that Holmes ignored Watson's warnings completely. In 1897 the latter observed of his friend, "The state of his health was not a matter in which he himself took the faintest interest, for his mental detachment was absolute".[9]

It may be urged that Watson should have been even more positive than he was in his warnings to Holmes. In his defence,

[1] *The Hound of the Baskervilles*, L., p. 322.　　　　[2] *Ibid.*, p. 299.
[3] *The Devil's Foot*, S., p. 1050.
[4] *The Man with the Twisted Lip*, S., p. 142–3.　　[5] *Silver Blaze*, S., p. 305.
[6] *The Dying Detective*, S., p. 1003.　　　[7] *The Five Orange Pips*, S., p. 116.
[8] *The Devil's Foot*, S., p. 1050.　　　　　　　[9] *Ibid.*, p. 1041.

however, it is fair to recall that as late as 1917 not all medical men considered that tobacco amblyopia caused total blindness, as I understand they now do. H. L. Eason, Senior Ophthalmic Surgeon at Guy's Hospital, for example, wrote at that time:

> "The Amblyopia due to Lead, Alcohol, Tobacco, Quinine or Atoxyl is usually described as toxic amblyopia, and the symptoms are somewhat similar in all the varieties . . . In tobacco amblyopia there is a central loss of vision for colours, green only in the earlier stages, subsequently green and red, and in extreme cases even a central Scotoma for white; total blindness is practically unknown. The patient states that he sees better in a dull than a bright light, and that he is incapable of reading and writing, or distinguishing silver from gold coins."[1]

In 1914 Holmes had been an exceptionally heavy smoker of shag for at least thirty-three years. This is firmly established by Watson's record of their conversation during their first meeting in 1881 at Barts, when they agreed to share rooms:

> " 'I have my eye on a suite in Baker Street', [Holmes] said, 'which would suit us down to the ground. You don't mind the smell of strong tobacco, I hope?'
> 'I always smoke "ship's" myself,' I answered."[2]

At this time Holmes was only twenty-nine, and his eyesight was phenomenally keen. It will be recalled that he and Watson were looking out of their first-floor window into Baker Street, and noticed "a stalwart, plainly-dressed individual who was walking slowly down *the other side of the street* [my italics], looking anxiously at the numbers. He had a large blue envelope in his hand, and was evidently the bearer of a message." Holmes instantly identified him as a "retired sergeant of Marines".[3] When this was proved to be true, Holmes told the astounded Watson that the first fact which led him to this conclusion was that "even across the street" he could see a blue anchor tattooed on the back of the messenger's hand, "that smacked of the sea".[4]

---

[1] *An Index of Differential Diagnosis of Main Symptoms by various Writers* (Second Edition, Bristol and London, 1917), p. 759. The General Editor was Herbert French, Senior Pathologist and Lecturer at Guy's Hospital. The first edition was published in March, 1912.   [2] *A Study in Scarlet*, L., p. 12.
[3] *Ibid.*, L., p. 24.     [4] *Ibid.*, p. 25.

In those early years, before the shag tobacco had begun its deadly work, Holmes was clearly proud of his remarkable powers of observation:

"I can never bring you to realise the importance of sleeves, the suggestiveness of thumb-nails, or the great issues that may hang from a bootlace."[1]

"By a man's finger-nails, by his coat-sleeve, by his boot, by his trouser-knees, by the callosities of his forefinger and thumb, by his expression, by his shirt-cuffs—by each of these things a man's calling is plainly revealed."[2]

"Never trust to general impressions, my boy, but concentrate yourself upon details. My first glance is always at a woman's sleeve. In a man it is perhaps better first to take the knee of the trouser."[3]

It is, of course, true that Holmes impressed upon Watson the sharp distinction between seeing and observing, which the latter had clearly failed to understand:

" 'I am baffled, until you explain your process. And yet I believe that my eyes are as good as yours.'

'Quite so', [Holmes] answered, lighting a cigarette, and throwing himself down into an arm-chair. 'You see, but you do not observe. The distinction is clear. For example, you have frequently seen the steps which lead up from the hall to this room.'

'Frequently.'

'How often?'

'Well, some hundreds of times.'

'Then how many are there?'

'How many! I don't know.'

'Quite so! You have not observed. And yet you have seen. That is just my point. Now, I know that there are seventeen steps, because I have both seen and observed.' "[4]

Nobody can cavil at Holmes's point, but he himself conceded in his last sentence that he had to see before he could observe. His excellent sight was an essential ingredient in these impres-

[1] *A Case of Identity*, S., p. 66.
[2] *A Study in Scarlet*, L., p. 20. Holmes wrote this sentence in 1881 in *The Book of Life*. Michael and Mollie Hardwick attribute it in error to *The Sign of Four* (*The Sherlock Holmes Companion*, London, 1962, p. 162) and thus to the year 1888.
[3] *A Case of Identity*, S., p. 66.    [4] *A Scandal in Bohemia*, S., p. 6.

sive demonstrations of his early years, as two examples make clear.

" 'My dear Mr. Grant Munro—', began Holmes. Our visitor sprang from his chair. 'What!' he cried. 'You know my name?'

'If you wish to preserve your *incognito*,' said Holmes, smiling, 'I should suggest that you cease to write your name upon the lining of your hat, or else that you turn the crown towards the person whom you are addressing.' "[1]

" 'You have come in by train this morning, I see.'

'You know me, then?'

'No, but I observe the second half of a return ticket in the palm of your left glove.' "[2]

In later years, it was a different story. In the sombre affair of the severed human ears, Holmes could still read without effort the heading of the account of the horrific experience of Miss Susan Cushing, "A GRUESOME PACKET" in the *Daily Chronicle*. The article itself, in small print and of some length, however, presented difficulties, and Holmes's request to Watson "Perhaps you would be good enough to read it aloud", was significant.[3] This was no coincidence, for in the Pycroft case Holmes did exactly the same thing. He could read the headlines of the *Evening Standard*, "CRIME IN THE CITY. MURDER AT MAWSON & WILLIAMS. GIGANTIC ATTEMPTED ROBBERY; CAPTURE OF THE CRIMINAL", but so far as the long account was concerned, he had to ask Watson to "kindly read it aloud to us".[4] The text of the Scott Eccles case suggests that this procedure of Holmes using Watson's eyes to save the strain on his own had become a matter of routine:

" 'THE OXSHOTT MYSTERY. A SOLUTION. ARREST OF SUPPOSED ASSASSIN.' Holmes sprang in his chair as if he had been stung when I read the head-lines.

'By Jove!' he cried. 'You don't mean that Baynes has got him?'

'Apparently,' said I, as I read the following report.' "[5]

[1] *The Yellow Face*, S., p. 337.
[2] *The Speckled Band*, S., p. 175.
[3] *The Cardboard Box*, S., p. 927.
[4] *The Stockbroker's Clerk*, S., p. 372.
[5] *Wisteria Lodge*, S., p. 909.

In the affair at Yoxley Old Place there was no real attempt at concealment in Watson's text as to the state of Holmes's eyes. The detective doggedly struggled to read an inscription on a palimpsest with the aid of "a powerful lens", presumably to pass the time during "a wild, tempestuous night towards the close of November", but was forced to desist. "It is trying work for the eyes", he told Watson bravely, as he laid the lens aside.[1] What a tragic change this was, we may think, from the days when Holmes's vision was such that he could read with the naked eye a tattoo mark on the hand of a man in motion on the opposite side of Baker Street.[2] No wonder that Watson could not hide the facts in his continuation of this sombre catalogue of the nemesis that was overtaking his unfortunate friend. John Hector McFarlane had brought with him the newspaper that contained the account of the presumed death of Jonas Oldacre, but Holmes knew that it was useless for him even to pretend to be able to read it:

"Our visitor stretched forward a quivering hand and picked up the *Daily Telegraph*, which still lay upon Holmes's knee.

'If you had looked at it, sir, you would have seen at a glance what the errand is on which I have come to you this morning.' "[3]

It seems possible that McFarlane may have guessed that Holmes's sight was now seriously defective, for although in acute distress and fearful of almost immediate arrest, he nevertheless found the place for Holmes and read the headlines to him:

"He turned it over to expose the central page. 'Here it is, and with your permission I will read it to you. Listen to this, Mr. Holmes. The headlines are: 'MYSTERIOUS AFFAIR AT LOWER NORWOOD. DISAPPEARANCE OF A WELL-KNOWN BUILDER. SUSPICION OF MURDER AND ARSON. A CLUE TO THE CRIMINAL.' "[4]

As we may by now expect, Holmes could do no other than appeal for assistance from his friend:

[1] *The Golden Pince-Nez*, S., p. 783. It may, of course, be urged that with the passing of the years Holmes had developed myopia, and that only his proud nature (*The Sussex Vampire*, S., p. 1180) prevented his wearing the spectacles he needed to correct his short sight. If this was so, one would have expected the use of a powerful lens to bring him more relief than it did. However, I concede the possibility that Holmes may have suffered from both myopia and the more deadly amblyopia.
[2] *A Study in Scarlet*, L., pp. 24–5.     [3] *The Norwood Builder*, S., p. 586.
[4] *Ibid.*, S., p. 586.

"We must use what time we have', said Holmes. 'Watson, would you have the kindness to take the paper and to read me the paragraph in question.'
Underneath the vigorous headlines which our client had quoted I read the following suggestive narrative."[1]

By 1914, what was clearly to be Holmes's eventual total blindness was obviously quite far advanced. Travel was now presenting practical difficulties, for it is noteworthy that in order to find his way safely to Von Bork's house Holmes had to send a telegram to Watson, whom he had not seen for several years, to take him in his motor car.[2] Watson waited dutifully outside while Holmes concluded his business with Von Bork, who imagined Watson merely to be "the chauffeur, a heavily built, elderly man, with a grey moustache [who] settled down, like one who resigns himself to a long vigil."[3] Apart from the necessary conveying of Holmes to and from his appointment ("Start her up, Watson, for it's time that we were on our way"[4]), indeed, Watson's role in the affair seems to have been limited to assisting Holmes to drink Von Bork's wine:

" 'Another glass, Watson!' said Mr. Sherlock Holmes, as he extended the bottle of Imperial Tokay. The thick-set chauffeur, who had seated himself by the table, pushed forward his glass with some eagerness.
'It is a good wine, Holmes.'
'A remarkable wine, Watson. Our friend upon the sofa has assured me that it is from Franz Joseph's special cellar at the Schoenbrunn Palace.' "[5]

The final proof of the condition of Holmes's eyes at this time, I feel sure, lies in the fact that it was evidently only at the closest quarters that he could now distinguish the beloved details of Watson's face. It is significant, it may be thought, that he had to take his old friend "by the shoulders",[6] so that their faces

---

[1] *The Norwood Builder*, S., pp. 586–7. "Read me" is suggestive. Clearly the fiction in one earlier example that Watson might have been reading aloud for the benefit of the client as well as for Holmes had been dropped.
[2] *His Last Bow*, S., p. 1081. We may think that with his disability Holmes would not have accepted the Van Bork case at all had the matter not been one of extreme national emergency.
[3] *Ibid.*, p. 1075.      [4] *Ibid.*, p. 1086.      [5] *Ibid.*, p. 1080.
[6] *His Last Bow*, S., p. 1081.

would be less than two feet apart, in order to see him. Even at this small distance, the fact that Watson was now in appearance an "elderly man, with a grey moustache"[1] was obviously unnoticed by Holmes:

"I've hardly seen you in the light yet. How have the years used you? You look the same blithe boy as ever."[2]

In my view, Holmes had been advised in 1914 that the deadly progress of the tobacco-amblyopia had gone too far to be reversed, and that in the near future he would be totally blind. If final proof is needed, it surely lies in the striking fact that in *His Last Bow*, alone amongst Watson's accounts of Holmes's cases, there is no mention of the detective smoking a pipe. Faced with the catastrophic verdict of the specialist he had finally been persuaded to consult, he had given up the habit in horror. We may think that the old clay pipe, together with its companions of briar and cherrywood,[3] had been thrown over the Sussex cliffs at high tide. We recall with sadness that "a half-smoked sodden cigar hung from the corner of his mouth" in 1914,[4] which tells its own story to anyone who has tried to give up the habit of cigarettes or a pipe. It was, of course, too late and Holmes knew that it was. We remember that Holmes was the logician who had always insisted to Watson that "all things should be seen exactly as they are".[5]

For my part, I believe that for Holmes, whose whole life had been devoted to the exercise of his remarkable and indeed unique powers of observation, the advent of complete blindness would be unbearable. He would know how to arrange matters competently when the time came. Even in the earliest years of Holmes's career Watson had recorded that his friend's knowledge of chemistry was "profound", and that he was "well up in belladonna, opium and poisons generally".[6] The end, I imagine, would be quite peaceful. Apart from the one insuperable problem of blindness, he had nothing to regret. In view of his remarkable memory, it is reasonable to suppose that he

[1] *His Last Bow*, S., p. 1075.        [2] *Ibid.*, p. 1081.
[3] This was the "long cherrywood pipe which was wont to replace his clay when he was in a disputatious rather than a meditative mood." (*The Copper Beeches*, S., p. 275).        [4] *His Last Bow*, S., p. 1076.
[5] *The Greek Interpreter*, S., p. 479.        [6] *A Study in Scarlet*, L. pp. 17–18.

would recall the grateful words of the courageous, dying John Turner, who had told Holmes that the latter's death-bed, when it came, would "be the easier for the thought of the peace which you have given to mine."[1]

I am aware that my reconstruction of these sombre events will at first cause sadness to many. Holmesian scholars are without exception men of high intelligence and sensitivity, however, and I therefore feel sure that on reflection they will share my view that if Holmes, kept alive by "royal jelly" or any other fanciful means, had really lived on until the middle of the twentieth century or later, he would inevitably have suffered indignities and embarrassments that no Sherlockian would care to contemplate. I refer, of course, to his financial circumstances.

I find it surprising that not one of the commentators who have suggested that Holmes may have lived to be 93, 103 or 108,[2] has given any consideration to the effect that inflation would have had upon the modest fortune of savings upon which the detective had retired in 1903. We know that he was not wealthy, for he himself told the Duke of Holdernesse that he was "a poor man"[3] as he patted his cheque affectionately and put it carefully into his pocket. He told Watson in 1891 that the services he had given to the Royal Family of Scandinavia and to the French Republic had finally made him independent, but only if he lived "in the quiet fashion" that was congenial to him.[4] The modesty of his savings is entirely to be expected, bearing in mind that he was only in practice for 23 years,[5] and that he frequently made no charge for his services.[6] In 1914 a cheque for £500 was of importance to him, for he told Watson that it "should be cashed early", before it was stopped.[7] If he had really lived on until the nineteen-fifties, we can be certain that the disastrous incline in the purchasing power of the income that had seemed adequate for his needs in 1903 would have made him a desperately poor man in his later years. We can be equally sure that

[1] *The Boscombe Valley Mystery*, S., p. 102.
[2] Mr. Alan Thomas has indignantly denied that Holmes has died at all and has suggested that when the proof that he is still alive becomes available those who have suggested otherwise "will do a Watson act—and faint". (*The Listener*, 4 October, 1962, p. 533).
[3] *The Priory School*, S., p. 696
[4] *The Final Problem*, S., p. 539.
[5] *The Veiled Lodger*, S., p. 1287.
[6] *Thor Bridge*, S., p. 1221.
[7] *His Last Bow*, S., p. 1086.

Holmes's "proud, self-contained nature"[1] would have prevented his acceptance of either private charity or assistance from the Ministry of Social Security.

Holmes was an enlightened man, and it seems fair to assume that he would consider that any individual has the right to end his life if existence has become insupportable. His old friend Edmund Gurney, who had been at Trinity College, Cambridge, with Holmes,[2] committed suicide in the Royal Albion Hotel, Brighton, in June, 1888, after his discovery of the wholesale frauds of spiritualism and psychical research, the subjects to which he had devoted six years of immense, unremitting labour in his capacity as the first Hon. Secretary of the Society for Psychical Research.[3] Holmes, like William James, was profoundly concerned over Gurney's death, as I have shown in my earlier study, and one wonders whether Holmes may not have been equally influenced by the entry for 5 August, 1889, in *The Diary of Alice James*, first published in 1894. Alice James was the sister of William James, and her brother knew well F. W. H. Myers and A. T. Myers and other prominent members of the S.P.R. Alice James's reference to the concealment of the suicide was clearly in regard to the highly misleading evidence given at the inquest by A. T. Myers.

"They say that there is little doubt that Mr. Edmund Gurney committed suicide. What a pity to hide it; every educated person who kills himself does something towards lessening the superstition."[4]

[1] *The Sussex Vampire*, S., p. 1180.
[2] "A College Friendship?", Hall, pp. 93–108.
[3] For an account of Gurney's life and death see my *The Strange Case of Edmund Gurney* (London, 1964).
[4] *The Diary of Alice James* (1965 edition, with an Introduction by Professor Leon Edel), p. 52.

# APPENDIX

# MEA CULPA

A NUMBER of my critics have properly pointed out that in my earlier book some documentation that was staring me in the face was omitted. Three examples are sufficient to illustrate this lack of knowledge or failure of memory on my part. I assembled some *obiter dicta* of Holmes to show that he thoroughly understood the mental processes and idiosyncracies of the gentler sex.[1] I forgot, of course, that he had pointed out that women never send reply-paid telegrams,[2] that in moments of agitation they fly to tea[3] and that "their most trivial action may mean volumes, or their most extraordinary conduct may depend upon a hairpin or a curling-tongs"[sic].[4]

In the account of Holmes's outstanding abilities as an actor,[5] I inexplicably overlooked the graceful compliment paid to him by Inspector Athelney Jones:

> "You would have made an actor, and a rare one. You had the proper workhouse cough, and those weak legs of yours are worth ten pounds a week."[6]

In demonstrating Holmes's extreme familiarity with life in the country,[7] I was exceedingly neglectful in failing to remember both the fact that he owned a hunting crop,[8] and the faithful Watson's rueful recording of Holmes's severe criticism of his report on the occupants of Charlington Hall, near Farnham in Surrey:

[1] Hall, p. 133–6.
[3] *The Crooked Man*, S., p. 449.
[5] Hall, p. 29.
[7] Hall, pp. 19–22.

[2] *Wisteria Lodge*, S., p. 892.
[4] *The Second Stain*, S., p. 872.
[6] *The Sign of Four*, L., p. 225.
[8] *A Case of Identity*, S., p. 74.

" 'You really have done remarkably badly. He returns to the house, and you want to find out who he is. You come to a London house agent!'

'What should I have done?' I cried, with some heat.

'Gone to the nearest public-house. That is the centre of country gossip. They would have told you every name, from the master to the scullery-maid." '[1]

In parenthesis it may be thought that Holmes was a trifle hard on poor Watson, who firmly believed that he "had done a fairly good morning's work",[2] when it is recalled that the great detective conceded to his biographer during a train journey to Tavistock that he himself had made a blunder, "which is, I am afraid, a more common occurrence than anyone would think who only knew me through your memoirs".[3] This confession was rather amply confirmed, we may think, by Holmes's observation to Watson in the matter of Mr. Neville St. Clair:

"I think, Watson, that you are now standing in the presence of one of the most absolute fools in Europe. I deserve to be kicked from here to Charing Cross."[4]

To return to the subject of my own frailties, Lord Donegall took me to task over an alleged mistake in his otherwise approving review of my book. He disagreed with my convinced opinion in regard to the location of Holmes's undergraduate years:

"Trinity College, Cambridge, says Mr. Hall, and his evidence, though constructed on quick-sands, is fleetingly impressive. But, as I proved, conclusively, many years ago, that Holmes was at Christ Church, Oxford, Mr. Hall's conclusions in this particular *Study* are irrelevantly misleading and can be relegated to an obscurity which no serious student should begrudge them!"[5]

These were harsh words, it may be thought, to use of the "skilful surveyor of highways and hedges"[6] and of Sherlock Road,

[1] *The Solitary Cyclist*, S., p. 648.
[2] *Ibid.*, p. 648.       [3] *Silver Blaze*, S., p. 307.
[4] *The Man with the Twisted Lip*, S., p. 143.
[5] *The Sherlock Holmes Journal*, Winter, 1969, p. 105.
[6] Harrison Ainsworth, *Rookwood* (London, 1834) p. 249.

Sherlock Close and the "row of ancient colleges" in Cambridge,[1] the solver of the curious incident of the Great Court and Quadrangle of Trinity,[2] the investigator of the problem of dogs in colleges[3] and, above all, the discoverer of the entry for "R. Musgrave" in *The Cambridge University Calendar* at the relevant date.[4] Privately, I may say that this fourth example of the kind of solid evidence I assembled in my book was in my view an advance in human knowledge that can properly be compared with the invention of the wheel. Like Holmes, "I cannot agree with those who rank modesty among the virtues."[5]

Since my position in the matter is obviously impregnable, and because Lord Donegall and I are good friends with many interests in common, I feel that in the circumstances an attitude of kindly and understanding tolerance is appropriate. There is no literary controversy, since in his review Lord Donegall finds himself unable to counter, or even to bring himself to mention, the formidable and indeed conclusive evidence for Trinity. This omission is of psychological interest, and we may suspect that in the single matter of Holmes's university and college Lord Donegall's view is uncharacteristically lacking in objectivity. Since he is committed to the claim that he has "proved conclusively, many years ago, that Holmes was at Christ Church Oxford" (Lord Donegall's own college), it is clear that I have inadvertently trodden on a pet corn. In these circumstances it is unfortunate that in my book I had something to say about Holmes's habit of indoor revolver practice from an armchair, and his adornment of "the opposite wall with a patriotic V.R. done in bullet-pocks."[6] I remarked:

> "It must be conceded that this was a most unusual and expensive habit, involving noise, general inconvenience and the frequent replastering and redecoration of the sitting room wall. One is entitled to wonder what was the provenance of the idea. I fear that the exponents of the now exploded theory that Holmes was at Christ Church, Oxford, may urge upon

[1] *The Creeping Man*, S., p. 1254 and Hall, pp. 80–2.
[2] *The Three Students*, S., pp. 767 and 773 and Hall, pp. 83–4.
[3] *The "Gloria Scott"*, S., p. 375 and Hall, pp. 74–6.
[4] *The Musgrave Ritual*, S., p. 399. "Reginald Musgrave had been in the same college as myself."
[5] *The Greek Interpreter*, S., p. 478.   [6] *The Musgrave Ritual*, S., p. 396.

us in desperation the pretty story, still extant, that the words *No Peel* in the door opposite the foot of the Hall stairway were executed in bullet-pocks by the third Duke of Northumberland at the time of the Corn Law repeal. Alas, for such a hope . . ."[1]

It is clear that a reviewer who is a Christ Church man would be unnecessarily provoked by the wording of the third sentence, and that it would therefore have been prudent of me to have remembered with sympathy Lord Donegall's sincere but mistaken views on this delicate subject.

[1] Hall, pp. 84–5. The third Duke was at St. John's College, Cambridge, and the fourth, who entered the Navy at the age of 13, did not attend a university. The words were *burnt* into the door in 1829 as an election slogan by the undergraduates of Sir Robert Peel's own college, as a protest against his return to Parliament as a burgess of the University after he had carried his Bill for the emancipation of Roman Catholics.

# INDEX OF CASES

# INDEX OF
# NAMES, PLACES AND PUBLICATIONS
(Sherlock Holmes, John H. Watson and Baker Street are not included)